With best wishes,

/ Walchars, ff

Splendor and Shadow

by

JOHN WALCHARS, S.J.

North Central Publishing Company
St. Paul, Minnesota

IMPRIMI POTEST: John V. O'Connor, S.J., Provincial, New England Province, Boston, June 1, 1963.
NIHIL OBSTAT: Andrew Martin, Censor librorum, August 1, 1963.
IMPRIMATUR: † Christopher J. Weldon, Bishop of Springfield, August 1, 1963.

Printed in the United States of America by the North Central Publishing Company, St. Paul, Minnesota.

by the same author

"The Call from Beyond"

242
WAS

Acknowledgments to Miss Carolina Accorsi and Mrs. Charles V. Ryan, Sr., for their great help and encouragement.

Gratefully dedicated

to

Mrs. Catherine Brenninkmeyer

Prefatory Note

Father John Walchars' reflections in this, his most recent book, are at once mellow and moving. In the tradition of the Ignatian method of meditation, they are directed toward the whole person, the intellect and the will, the faculties of sense and of soul, the spiritual and psychological levels of the person at prayer. As a result, they are useful to one eager to profit fully from the thinking in the heart which is the essence of a good Retreat.

The themes of these meditations are as old as meditation itself; this is as it should be. The insights that Father Walchars brings to these themes have a freshness born of the feeling with which the priestly author writes. They have a cogency springing from the spiritual wisdom, ever ancient, ever new, which he brings to his writing.

New ways, new emphases, new directions will influence the Retreat Movement, as they are influencing all things else in the life of the Church. Many of these are long overdue and they will be of lasting significance; some will have their little hour of novelty and, having desirably stimulated the abiding interests, will pass their way. In any case, whatever the new types of approach to the central business of the Closed Retreat, meditative writing of the basic, perennial kind with which Father Walchars is so much at home will always be indispensible. *Splendor and Shadow* will have a permanent, welcome place in the libraries of Retreat Houses and among the books cherished by devout retreatants.

✠ John Wright
BISHOP OF PITTSBURGH

Table of Contents

SPLENDOR AND SHADOW

ONE

Who Am I?

The astonishing wisdom of the Greek philosopher has found for man a name which expressed so perfectly the stark reality of his existence that the Christian philosopher could do no better than to repeat what he has learned from the antiquity. Homo est animal rationale — man is a rational animal. So it was stated and so it echoed through the centuries right into the lecture halls of our days where our youth strives hard to learn much more about the never-ending mystery of our species.

A twofold mirror opens up before the eyes of man and both directions show the human countenance. A beast he is, no doubt, with all the fury of the jungle in his seething blood, and a mind he possesses as brilliant as the sparkle of the star on our sky. He returns to the source of the soil whenever his hunger and thirst announce their presence and he gazes to the Heavens above the moment his mind presents to him a higher destiny. Like powerful streams, these dissenting powers pitch against the shores of life challenging man to accept the terms of exuberant growth, or to submit to the conditions of a merciless destruction. Engaged in this titanic struggle which tears apart all peace and harmony, man has to know that he is born for strife and not for rest: "Do not imagine that I have come to bring peace to the earth; I have come to bring a sword, not peace." Ruins mark the lusty steps of violence while majestic spires proclaim the touch of the genial master. Saint and sinner, both, man has fathered, and either one is dialed from the numbers of his set.

The carnal and the spiritual, the instincts and the mind, as different as they might seem, are guests at the same banquet. Like roaring lions they stalk over the field of life, refusing to be accommodated or dismissed until the one has conquered the promise of the other. Slight achievements are just as well accepted as the price of total victory: "Nature is crafty and draws away many; she ensnares and deceives them, and always has self for her end. But grace walks with simplicity, turns aside from all appearance of evil, offers no deceits, and does all things purely for God." [1]

Man pays his debts with a two-pictured coin. On the one side of the coin he sees the face of God, whom he wishes so dearly to serve, and on the other side he sees his own desires, which he loves so much. Torn between the two, man's life is strained with risks. His very fate is insecure, and until the very last minute of his precarious existence, no one can guarantee that he is safe. Uncertainty accompanies his steps as shadows accompany the golden rays of our sun. The leap of the beast however is secure. Propelled by the power of the instincts only, the animal never fails. Man has no doubts about the fate of the lamb in the claws of a rapacious tiger, nor do we blame the bird for a wrong song. We know that their performance is a must and that they obey a script which was conceived and written by a greater master. The fate of man is different; his life is never fixed. Through his performance he is forever his own free agent. Not that he is liberated from the stormy drives of lust and hatred, nor are his passions numb or cold, but other powers reign in him which make him strong enough to tame the passions to his will. Not instincts only are his inheritance, but intelligence and will are added parcels to his crib: "Thus, brethren, nature has no longer any claim upon us, that we should live a life of nature. If you live a life of nature, you are marked out for death; if you mortify the ways of nature through the power of the Spirit, you will have life." [2]

[1] I. X. 3. 54.
[2] Rom. 8. 12–14. (According to R. Knox)

2

Our instincts and their outbursts are of equal goodness or malice as the mind behind the scene. In themselves they are just as much a masterpiece of God as the wings of angels. The guidance which inspires them makes the difference and determines whether they turn into a fearful avalanche or into a hallowed blessing. Not that we deny the vitality and force of our hungry instincts, — we know too well how fierce their threat can be, — but it would be wrong to label them as wild or dangerous, since of themselves they wish to serve and are unruly only by the order of the higher powers of the soul. Whatever man is, he is on account of the strength of his mind and not on account of the appeal of his natural appetites and cravings. Instincts are like beautiful instruments. The touch of the genius creates the wonder of brilliant melodies and rhythms whereas the clumsy fingers of the amateur bring forth a boring listless discord. As we blame not the instrument for the difference, so can we not reproach the instincts for defeats or triumphs. A man might use his body to commit a sin, but mind and will are the culprits who chart the act of sinning: "Who can unravel that complex twisted knottedness? It is unclean, I hate to think of it or look at it. I long for Thee, O Justice and Innocence, Joy and Beauty of the Clear of sight, I long for Thee with unquenchable longing. There is sure repose in Thee and life untroubled. He that enters into Thee, enters into the joy of his Lord and shall not fear and shall be well in Him who is the Best. I went away from Thee, my God, in my youth I strayed too far from Thy sustaining power, and I became to myself a barren land." [3]

The intimate partnership of mind and will issues enough securities and guarantees to keep the rolling stream of instincts under firm and tight control. Not that we deny that there are naughty fugitives who cunningly escape detection and enjoy some frolics of their own, but their number is irrelevant and never constitutes the whole of human nature. Mental stress and bodily fatigue might diminish the alert and allow some instincts to stroll around unchecked and free, but from common intuition and experience we know that such drives — irresistible as they may seem — are not the ordinary diet of a healthy, wholesome being. Even the "unconscious," as modern and as profitable as its name is dressed today, has not the power to destroy the eternal responsibility of mind and will. Its knowl-

[3] Conf. 2. 10.

ledge might induce us to judge more leniently another man's defeat, but it will never absolve us from the obligation to give an account to God about the deeds we have performed. It might be good perhaps to remember that behind the mysterious veil of the "unconscious" many insincerities, ugly habits and greedy dreams try to hide their face and continue to exist without a real existence. Those who do not coerce their desires soon will be the victims of their cravings and, being unable to face the mirror of their guilt, become anxious to flee into the saving darkness of the unconscious. Wisdom only, paired with calm sincerity, is able to decide which is which: "You must be quit of the old self, and the habits that went with it; you must be clothed in the new self, that is being refitted all the time for closer knowledge, so that the image of God, who created it is its pattern." [4]

To take a purely natural outlook on man could easily induce us to take a pessimistic view about his inner strength and valor. It seems to be one thing to possess principles and it seems to be another thing to live by them. After all we only have to look over the battlefield of our own heart and we discover there quickly many a ruin or even shameful disasters which we have created "in spite of our better knowledge." How well do we understand the sharpminded apostle Paul, when he confessed so sincerely: "The law, as we know, is something spiritual; I am a thing of flesh and blood, sold into the slavery of sin. My own actions bewilder me; what I do is not what I wish to do, but something which I hate." [5] What a great consolation for us to know that this great apostle performed deeds which he hated and in spite of all that, still found a triumphant place on our altar. How did he ever do it? Not alone, to be sure, but with the help from above. The assurance from revelation that God's grace is sufficient for him and that our Lord would never allow him to be tempted beyond his strength, this conviction gave him the dynamic power which achieved such surprising results. Gratia Dei sum, quod sum — through the grace of God, I am what I am — he gladly admitted and he meant what he said. We too are eager to believe in this celestial promise of comfort and strength; otherwise, we could never speak of Christian heroism or demand at

[4] Col. 3. 9–10.
[5] Rom. 7. 14–15.

4

times fidelity to the teaching of Christ at the price of heroic sacrifices. Such demands would be hard to understand and justify, unless we are sure that we can count on God's marvelous help in our
special difficulties: "At the present time we move towards doing
good, since our heart has so conceived by Your Spirit; but at an
earlier time we moved towards doing ill, for we have gone away
from you. But you, God, who alone are good have never ceased to
do good. Some indeed of our works are good through Your grace,
but they are not eternal. After them we hope that we shall find rest
in the greatness of your sanctification." [6]

Man has to admit that he is never at his best if he allows his mind
to follow blindly the alluring dictates of sensual drives and powers.
To bend his mind in order to conform and please the cravings of
the appetite and to do only what his senses like, such a performance
is not only second rate but it also creates an image of man which
does not correspond to his real identity. If he hearkens to only one
voice — his natural desires — and deafens his ear to the murmurs of
his better knowledge, he makes a puppet of himself at the mercy of
his ever-craving lust and passions. He can not enjoy his real self
since he is never sure what his wild and reckless hunger demands
from him next. Like a ship without a captain, he is at the mercy of
the stormy waves of thirst and hunger, and soon — all too soon —
he will be drowned in the mud of his perversions: "I could not distinguish the white light of love from the fog of lust. Both love and
lust boiled within me, and swept my youthful immaturity over the
precipice of evil desires to leave me half drowned in a whirlpool
of abominable sins. Your wrath had grown mighty against me and I
knew it not. I had grown deaf from the clanking of the chain of my
mortality, the punishment for the pride of my soul: and I departed
further from You and You left me to myself." [7]

A beautiful alternative is up for choice. In his never-ending quest
for the melody of happiness, man can search deeply in his mind,
break open the deafness of his heart, and hearken to another
voice in his restless soul, the voice of reason, so much enlightened by
the grace of God. To follow this superior lead and act against the
hunger of his wily instincts, this is the mark of man, which sets him up

[6] Conf. 13. 38.
[7] Conf. 2. 2.

against the pack of greedy wolves. Not just to cleave to the seams of life for the sensual pleasures it peddles away in the darkness of its soul, but to seek life in the spirit of a relentless and fearless discoverer refusing to rest until the secrets of the earth are conquered, this alone makes life worth living. The hero in this drama needs no mask. He wears his real identity and spells his name as God has written it in all eternity. As martyrs die for the sake of living and suicides vanish for the sake of dying, so does a man of reason develop life to its full bloom, while gluttons in their fleshly cravings are hunting life to death. The man who has taken out an insurance not to safeguard his personal treasures but to secure his own identity, this is the man who is rich even if he is a pauper. Being firmly guided in his steps, he is no longer a play-toy of the fleeting minutes, nor is he open to all the risks of life, changing with the stronger blows of wind. Firmly established in his own inner conviction and irrevocably fixed in his relation to his holy faith, he can walk through darkness as safely as through light. He has found a secret which those immersed in pleasures will never taste or know: "Blessed is the man, who for Thee, O Lord, lets go all things created; who offers violence to his nature, and through fervor of spirit crucifies the lusts of the flesh: that so, his conscience being cleared up, he may offer to Thee pure prayer, and may be worthy to be admitted among the choir of the angels, having excluded all things of the earth both from without and within." [8]

The modern man is lonely. Abandoned by God whom he does not seek, he finds a self he only recognizes as a total stranger. Even in speaking to himself he conceals his voice and while laughing sheds his tears. One island only is left for him to flee to, the island of despair. Surrounded by his brilliant technical achievements, which serve him all the thrills he wants, he feels abandoned and alone as no man ever felt before in history, much like the child who is encompassed by a heap of shiny playtoys but can not enjoy them because he is blind. After all the brilliant mastery of learning in which the modern man excels, he has to begin to unlearn again and return to the sources which he betrayed. The mask of the pagan hero which grew so well to his lusty face is growing narrow and so cold that he begins to hate its empty and elusive promise. His pagan morals which

[8] I. X. 3. 48.

he believed so far beyond the Christian revelation all of a sudden show their claws and threaten him with total war and mass destruction. A paradise on earth he dreamed of and hell on earth is in the making. To allow one idea to grow too weak permits the other idea to grow too strong. By taking God away from all the avenues of mind, the idea "self" began to grow in such proportions that it overshadowed every other thought of mind. Yet, as we know so well, no other tyrant is so cruel as the tyranny of self. So is he eating his own food, although it never stills his piercing hunger: "And I put the question, supposing we were immortals and could live in perpetual enjoyment of the body without any fear of loss, why we should not then be happy, or what else should we seek. I did not realize that it belonged to the very heart of my wretchedness to be so drowned and blinded in it that I could not conceive that light of honor, and of beauty loved for its own sake, which the eye of the flesh does not see but only the innermost soul." [9]

A man in danger may save his life by risking it with a death defying leap. A captive surrounded by an iron net of enemies might reach his precious freedom by the most daring break through his oppressors. To cleave to life and wait until the fire of courage dies away have never helped a perilous escape. Only to wait for death produces nothing but a coward.

Modern man is in the same predicament. He can choose precious freedom or remain imprisoned by the chains of his own lust. Of the two decisions one must be his own. If he resolves to stay a slave to his unruly instincts, obscenity will be declared an art and filth will bloom in the disguise of literary merits. Sordid pictures as long as they are a thumping financial hit will top the list of entertainments. Vulgarity will gradually become the law of the land. If he decides however to turn his soul to life and liberty, a brilliant future is within his reach. At first his inner discipline has to mature, since this is the virtue which makes all other virtues grow. What use is a man who could govern the world but can not rule his own restless mind? Discipline is not an enemy of freedom as license of behaviour is not a proof of it. Freedom's greatness is always tested by the power we possess to rule the mind. Real life is order, without the need to impose a sword. To act according to what we conceive as right and to refuse to

[9] Conf. 6. 16.

be influenced by likes and dislikes, this is the test discipline must pass. There are many areas left in life to which no "must" signs are attached and wherein we recognize the challenge of tomorrow. This area, as wide perhaps as our mighty mountains, is in the reach of man who harnesses his own powers. Not that we imply that discipline will be rewarded with more influence or money — it might well stay poor — but we assert that it brings self-respect and honor. To possess well regulated centers in our hearts preserves us at least from being pushed through life like idiots or slaves. How much more conducive it is to make self-discipline a source of happiness in life, than to bear with the vicissitudes of life as something which has to be endured like rain.

Homo est animal rationale — man is an animal endowed with reason. To subdue the cunning powers of the beast and bend its vital forces to the might of will, this is the challenge man must accept through the entire span of his existence. Those amongst us who master this challenge the best deserve to wear the crown.

8

TWO

How Strong Is My Mind

There are many amongst us who freely acknowledge the awe-inspiring power of God and willingly submit to the benevolent rule which guides the stars of the heavens and nourishes the growing life on earth. Yet we might easily forget that there exists a similar power in our universe, a power so strong that no one will ever be able to conquer it nor mighty enough to banish it. This is the power of the human mind. Free like the pitching waves of the ocean, the mind can break the bars of the mightiest fortress, and dynamic like the force of an avalanche, it can easily bend the sword of the most ferocious warrior. So great a strength it possesses that every threat which seeks to enforce a limit to the endless horizons is surely defeated and condemned to wither away in a stony desert.

The great ones amongst us will never hesitate to reckon with the imperishable force of ideas since they are ready to pay honor to the freedom of the human genius. The little ones, however, call them dictators or leaders, will never cease to try to put irons and chains on the restless wings of our intellectual conquests and poison the very roots from which real greatness can arise. It seems to be an irresistible temptation for the weaklings in history to erase the brilliant achievements of human wisdom and substitute for it their own

9

silly schemes. At times they succeed, especially if they use their cunning brutality and apply their savage injections. They might even cheer themselves into their easy victories only to find out in the bitter end that they have challenged a force far greater than their colossal empires and far more eruptive than their most hideous weapons. Many a battle in history was lost because a bloody sword revolted against the power of an idea and often a crusade was won, even against insuperable odds, because the human genius broke through the chain of terror and found again its precious freedom.

Man might be able to harness the eruptive powers of a vulcano; man might even try to tame the assault of an avalanche but he will forever fail in his attempt to coerce the power of the human mind. A straightjacket can only strangle the unruly motions of a tormented body but it can never extinguish truth. Man must think to remain a man. Take this precious endowment away from him and what is left is a beast, so cruel a beast that you can find no equal to it in our steaming jungles.

Our civilization — thousands of years old — is only a prodigious manifestation of the relentless drive of the human genius. It did not come into existence at once; it grew and developed like any other seed thrown into the furrow of centuries. A long road led from the cruel forests and primitive caves to the launching of our missiles and to the thrust of our rockets. Man had to learn first how to use stones, with a few edges chipped off so as to fit the rough palm of his hairy hand; then better stones were chosen which were sliced, sharpened and rounded until they were efficient, attractive and even beautiful. The habit of cutting stones soon grew into a craft and even into a tradition and with the growing tradition, a refinement developed in the human mind which created our first masterpieces.

With the stone age vanishing, inventions followed inventions. The flame of fire was commanded, earth was magically changed into hard, endurable crockery and at last metal, sharp glittering metal flashed under the brilliant rays of a triumphant sun. The barbarian was transformed into a civilized man who gradually established himself as the undisputed ruler of the universe. The beasts in the forests found their master. Rightly could the Psalmist sing to his harp: "What is man that thou shouldst remember him? What is Adam's breed, that it should claim thy care?

Thou hast placed him only a little below the angels crowning him with glory and honour, and bidding him rule over the works of thy hands.

Thou has put them all under his dominion, the sheep and the cattle, and the wild beasts besides; the birds in the sky, and the fish in the sea, that travel by the sea's paths.

O Lord, our Master, how the majesty of thy name fills all the earth!" [1]

It would be wrong to imply that our civilization is without blemish. No doubt, it carries like every piece of human creation, the vexing stigmatas of frailty and imperfection. As the vast and turbulent sea, the genius in man rides so often the crest of the waves only to be pitched again and wounded by the sharp edged cliffs on the nearby shore. Brilliant heights have so often changed into periods of depressive corruption and utter debasement. Turnabouts like that might enter the pages of history unexpectedly and at times so swiftly that even the most powerful nations are swept by it into oblivion. The Roman Empire with its well-groomed Caesar and disciplined legions was only ONE lost pawn in the never finished game between corruption and resurrection. Other nations, less known and more easily forgotten, have shared the same doom. It was however not the sword, as dangerous as it might be, which crushed the might of an idea nor was it the ugly threat of persecution but the poisonous sting of wealth and sensual pleasures which proved to be the greatest menace to the survival of the mind. Soft thrills and not brutal violence dealt the ruthless blow to the roots of a great civilization. Yet even amongst so many tombstones the idea survived. Even after the destruction of the Roman Empire when the bridges were ruined, the harbors burned, the drains choked, the libraries ransacked, the might of the idea refused to yield. It stayed alive perhaps in a hidden monastery or in a scholar's hideout where a patient monk or a brilliant scholar preserved the mighty past and handed it over faithfully into the begging hands of a new generation. A culture which has lost its speech has found expression again.

[1] Ps. 8. 5–10.

The situation in our days has not altered the message to any decisive degree. As we are not born thoughtful or thoughtless but make ourselves what we are, so has our civilization created its own particular image. Our scientists enjoy an exalted position which some even like to credit with ultimate faith. Unlimited fortunes are placed before their magnificent minds to make it possible for their daring dreams to burst into exuberant life. In complicated laboratories, in experimental studies, in testing new chemicals, in analyzing the mysterious rays of the cosmos, the genius in our generation wrestled more secrets from the tomb of nature than any other scientists in previous centuries. Our wings fly faster than the wings of sound; our missiles are ready, like the arrow of the hunter, to spear the glittering stars and mighty spaceships are constructed to land on the surprised face of our mysterious moon. Copious harvest eased the threat of hunger; diseases lost their sting of death and prodigious achievements lightened the burden of many daily chores. Paradise on earth will soon be our permanent guest, so it seems, and our days might turn into the happiest days human mankind ever witnessed.

Yet, something seems to be missing! Even in our most exalted hour when we seem to touch the garments of the sky we realize so deeply that we are not gods, nor are we like the angels except in fleeting seconds when we catch a little of the eternal wisdom and love someone who despises us. We know perhaps now, in the delirium of our triumphant conquests, that the scientist alone can not save us. We have to admit, some perhaps with bitter disappointment, that even the most brilliant genius remains a paradox, a contradiction of good and of evil, with no more power in his fingers than the child in his crib. The eternal question "what is truth?" has to be answered from above. If we presume to answer it alone, we not only crucify God again but with him we nail our own existence to a gallows which does not proclaim redemption but ruin and destruction. The coin of history is in our hands again. On one side of this coin we find the imprint of our brilliant accomplishments and on the other side of this coin we find the footprints of the lusty Roman. Which side will prevail? It is not easy to issue a reply to this thorny question. Some seem to be convinced that the chase after money and the drink of pleasure have such a strong grip on our soul that it will unavoidably strangle the mind and corrupt our heritage. They

12

claim that our lust and our riches which ridicule nobility and heroism will write the last chapter in the most pompous funeral in history. With a tragic undertone T. S. Eliot writes, "There were decent godless people. Their only monument the asphalt road and a thousand golf balls." [2] It is not unthinkable that the human mind can strangle its own life as Judas strangled his breath on a tree. It is not impossible that in spite of our floods of artificial lights the human spark will extinguish.

Last, but not least, another escape is cunningly offered to the intelligence of man, the escape into control. To force the dreams of man into a cold and narrow pattern and to compel the mind into a dark and empty alley, this is the brutal aim of so many in our critical and decisive days. No doubt this has been tried before in history but it was never so brutally devised — perhaps with the help of glittering needles — as in the practice of Communism. Here the mind of man ceases to be a mind and becomes part of a machine which has to be carefully geared, oiled and replaced when it begins to squeak. The free mind with its inner dynamic irrepressible force is cruelly exchanged with the tongue of a dummy who willingly stammers and repeats what others have shouted in his dulled and weary ears. The threat of the monolithic monsters is casting its evil shadow over our ill-prepared orbit. Their purpose is clearly defined; first, they establish one single explanation of the world which they proudly call pure evolutionism; then, they invent one single system of thought and action which they name dialectic materialism, and as their last final step they wish to enforce this cursed philosophy on the mind of everyone. Their fatal grip into the mind of man is so much like tearing up from their very roots all the beautiful flowers in God's world wide garden and substituting for all this sparkling variety one artificial flower and declaring it the best of all.

Since the success of Communism is often proportioned to the degree of ignorance, it triumphs more today than in days gone by. Proclaiming that their final victory is inevitable, a statement which they never proved, they find it rather easy to sway the mind of those who have ceased to think. Confused, like any flock without a shep-

[2] T. S. Eliot, *The Rock, Collected Poems 1909–1935*, New York, Harcourt, Brace & Co., 1952. Page 103.

herd, crowds follow the brighter promises and since the Communists predict that the grass will be greener and greener on their side of the fence, their flock is growing and growing.

The danger can not be minimized. More and more men allow their minds to shrink into the frame of a dictated formula and quite a number of them have settled down to live like well-trained animals ready to dance gingerly to the tune of their very pleased masters. We witness today the rare spectacle of whole nations turning into a noisy circus without a tent.

Where will it end? We do not know yet, but we have to ask ourselves the following questions: Are we strong enough to check the tide? Is there enough courage in our hearts to push back the waves which pitch so ferociously against the shores of our blessed continent? Must the whip first slash our own skin before it loses its deadly sting?

Outside the harbor of our greatest city a huge statue rises from the weary waves into the blue of a hopeful sky. This statue is not dedicated to the memory of a famous poet nor does it remind us of the noble deeds of a fearless warrior; it presents to our continent and to the whole world an idea — freedom. This idea, the symbol of our unconquered nation, has to stay aflame not only in the tongues of our brilliant orators, or in the secluded cells of our gifted writers but in the heart of every child, man and woman born under the roof of our cherished nation. We have to convince a puzzled world that the human genius, if FREE, creates the greatest wonders. It is up to us to prove that we are ready again, as so often before in history, to pay the highest price for the sake of freedom — our life. Prophets and poets have spoken enough about it; deeds are requested now. History never accepts substitutes nor do we need substitutes. We are prepared to accept our destiny and strong enough to face our responsibility. Perhaps some of us have to change our prayer from "Oh Lord, give me more money" to "Oh Lord, give me more wisdom." This is not impossible to achieve. Others may have to cleanse their hurried minds from the blight of modern materialism which has so successfully invaded our means of entertainment and the medium of public information. This can be accomplished too. Then will we discover again perhaps, even to our own surprise, that the genius

14

in the current of our soul has not yet vanished nor has the brilliant mind which made our nation so majestic fled from our midst.

Amongst the most impressive celebrations of our glorious faith is the commemoration of the descent of the Holy Ghost into our own frail, little world. Although the spirit of God, who draws order, form and beauty out of chaos, is far beyond our finite way of thinking, we still reserve for him a special place of honor and devotion in our memories and our prayers. On the calendar the feast of Pentecost is marked with strong and beautiful letters reminding us to celebrate this great event with a solemnity and splendor which is reserved for our greatest guest on earth.

More than ever before in the history of mankind we need the tremendous gifts which the Spirit from above dispenses so gracefully amongst its faithful children; more than ever before we have to beg for the light from the shores of eternity to scatter the darkness of our ignorance and disperse the shadows of our confusion. The mind of man creates the greatest wonders if it is influenced and guided by the wisdom which is divine.

Let us fall down into the dust from which we are made and to which we will return and pray from the depths of our whole mind,

> veni pater pauperum,
> veni dator munerum,
> veni lumen cordium.
> O, come, Thou father of the poor
> O, come, Thou source of our gifts,
> O, come, Thou Light of our hearts.

THREE

Who Is He

Whenever a man is set to talk about some problems or speaks about demands and orders, he can with ease and comfort employ the endings of the plural and use the pronouns "we and us" instead of saying "I and me." We are so used to this grammatical procedure that we are taking it in stride and no concern is shown by those who have to make decisions. They are so well aware of situations which are a problem not to one but surely to many, as they are usually advised of critical positions which are a thorn in many eyes. But if we speak about the wide world of the next one and look into relations we have with our friends the safety of the plural has to disappear and the lonely singular, the I, sharpened in its focus, surges to the lonely forefront and takes the full responsibility alone. Not that we assert we never meet a throng or influence a multitude, but such a meeting usually revolves around the outskirts of the human heart and leaves the center free and unperturbed. Meeting eye to eye with friends and enemies makes our love and hatred rise to an intensity which claims the total personality of man. No one but me will face the challenge of the other person, as no one but me can be its blessing or its curse. This responsibility can not be shared with others, since

16

I can not divide my heart much more than once: "Blessed is the man that loves Thee, O God, and his friends in Thee, and his enemy for Thee. For he alone loses no one that is dear to him, if all are dear in God, who is never lost." [1]

Rare is the fascinating beauty of the peaks of our mighty mountains which reach with their colossal strength into the snow-white pillows of the clouds just awakened at the arrival of the misty dawn. Majestic is the view of our roaring sea which surges and recoils with boundless inner confidence and fury, only to lie down again with such a meekness and a peace, as if it never dreamt of violence in its ferocious gale and laughter. Enchanting is the colorful delight of our pretty flowers which sprinkle with their innocence and perfume the face of our lovely meadows, as our golden stars embellish with their glitter the walls of our endless skies.

Can anything compare with this delightful array of nature's grandeur and of beauty?

Can anything be more impressive than all the majesty of nature's glory and magnificence?

Can anything be more beloved than this spectacular parade of splendor and of grace?

Is there such a thing?

Yes, there is.

Man!

For man, God has more room in his heart than for all our mountains, lakes and flowers; for man, God has far more concern in his thought than for all the colors of the seasons: "What is man that thou shouldst remember him? What is Adam's breed, that it should claim thy care? Thou hast placed him only a little below the angels, crowning him with glory and honour, and biding him rule over the works of thy hands." [2]

Man is declared by God HIS favorite. My agreement or my disagreement will only influence my own position but never alter God's surprising taste. To wish that my religion would be a heavenly affair between the Lord and me alone is purely a dream we entertain, if we are disappointed with the man God likes. If some still hope to find their Master, while waiting timidly behind a fence, they follow an illusion which they most gladly cherish and

[1] Conf. 4. 9.
[2] Ps. 8. 5–7.

pursue when others need their help and love. The very instant I was taken in by God as member of the human family, I was forbidden to choose convenient neutrality which hoists the flag of defeatism before it seriously thinks of help and action. Excessive haste is also frowned upon as it could be a clever camouflage of my desire to escape my call to succor and to aid the need of the abandoned. Nothing less than my complete attention seems to satisfy the ruling of the Lord: "Bear the burden of one another's failings; then you will be fulfilling the law of Christ." [3] To stop and see how deeply I have to bend to reach the wound I can heal, this is the only trademark of our new redemption, the only road worthy of my great dignity and honor. Everything else is a step back into darkness from which we were released through Christ's death on the cross.

While God has never attached distinctive elements to man, we supplement them with a vigor and a zeal as if we tried to make up for some deficiencies in God's eternal dream. Where God demanded only love, we introduce a "more or less," according to a grading which we ourselves so cleverly concocted in our ugly moods of pride and glory. Like little children we seek the tiny elements in which we differ and build them up to such tremendous heights that soon we can not see the face of man again. True greatness will forever reverse such hostile trends and restore to man its dignity and eminence, in spite of differences in religion and in color. As long as such nobility of mind and heart prevails in the soul of our nation we have the hope that God in his tremendous mercy will not abandon our land, in spite of our clumsy disappointment and our ugly failures. May we remember that the eyes of the whole world are on our shores today, judging our deeds much more than listening to our declarations.

If we detect in God's commanding voice a gentle predilection, it is no doubt for our poor. Without banalities or platitudes Christ solemnly declared that our beggars are the most beloved citizens in the streets of his eternal kingdom. So little now they call their own, only to own so much the moment when it counts. It was not laziness which God has glorified in his historic sermon on the mount but poverty which comes to us as a sequel of injus-

[3] Gal. 6. 2.

18

tices, imposed by use of brutal force or threats of laws and regulations. God never preached a bloody revolution against the might of riches, but he made it unmistakably clear that he demands a justice which secures for everyone enough to live in decency and honor. If many in our blessed nation, in spite of all determined efforts and endeavors, still have to live in want and desolation because a few are free to reap too much of our harvests, justice is still far away from our shores and peace will fail to plant its seed in our nation. Progress has been achieved, no doubt, in notable proportions but a long road is still ahead of us, a road so full of dangers and temptations that only love can march it to its blessed end. Communism as a voice speaks from the throat of demons. If we fail to recognize this demon, we only have to blame ourselves. But is not Communism more often just an echo of a word which could not find another lip to speak? Men and women, who finally grew desperate of hunger and misery, took fate in their own hands and sold their soul to a fanatic bidder who promised much and gave so little. They linked their disappointed dreams to a fallacious promise of a paradise on earth where all will surely receive so much that they will never starve or be in want again. Since they really had not much to lose, they gambled on the risk of gaining, only to find out so quickly, that they lost the little which they still possessed.

To glee over their tragic failure and accuse them of their faithless mind, without admitting our own responsibility and guilt, would frustrate thoroughly the bitter lesson we should finally begin to learn. The rich man of today is faced with two alternatives: to subdue his ugly greed and return at last to justice or to continue to worship his ever growing profits until he drowns in his own hunger. From his response it will depend whether the world will gain a new lease on love and on prosperity, or tumble deeply into chaos, from which it never might return: "Innocence, ill endowed, has the better of the wicked in their abundance; soon fails the strength of their arms, and still the Lord has the just in his keeping." [4]

The commanding voice of God might have been calm and strong when he called man into his existence, but the resulting

[4] Ps. 36. 16–17.

echo of his dramatic order is often so insignificant and small that we have difficulties to love and cherish what God presents to us as his beloved gift. We know that God looked over what he made and found it good and beautiful, and we do not intend to quarrel with the unexpected taste of the divine, but it is still at times so hard for us to understand God's wise decision, if we look back on our own experience. Man can be great and powerful, no doubt, and yield tremendous credit to his maker, since any famous masterpiece excels the name of its composer, but man can also be so little and so shameless that we would like just to forget at times the noble dignity of his creation. As you have ordered us, we walk quite brave and gentle towards your favorite children willing to share with them those precious gifts which you have strewn so generously on our path of life. But look, O Lord, what kind of strange receptions we receive. Some, it is true, appreciate the golden rays of our heart and receive our gifts with gratitude and joy, but see all others who do not care at all for us or our kindness but display a coldness and indifference which make us sad and bitter. None of your other creatures, nor even hunger, thirst and sufferings, can wound us so deeply as your friends can.

It really is not easy to give a just appraisal of your friends, O Lord, nor is it always pleasant to deal with men you find so lovable and precious. Men seem to be more of a mixture of things of good and evil, not really black or white but grayish mostly in their color. Even in the smaller things of life, which rarely are of importance, man can reveal a dignity and charm which even stun a pessimist only to reverse his kindness moments later into a selfishness and greed which puzzle even optimists. No man is only bad, they tell us, and we gladly nod approval, since we discovered often behind the zone of meanness and of violence a tender field of dignity and honor. Even in the most abandoned human being, who looks so desperate and bare, we might discover something warm and touching, which is so quietly great and innocent that we admit that we are moved by its impression. But what, O Lord, should we see first, the darkness or the light? What should we remember most in our weary moments, man's pride or his humility? We know that if we looked only deep enough we would have found in every man the vestige of your greatness, but we have stopped so often earlier, before we reached your sacred entrance, and all we found was human misery and greedy passions.

So it remains that if we look at man as just another animal, he is a sorry sight with only few attractions to his credit but if we see your countenance, O Lord, reflected in his being, man is at once the mightiest king in all of your creation. Since any song is bearable and even beautiful, if at the end all dissonant harmonies catch each other's breath to rest in one triumphant melody, so is the life of man a glorious success if after all his trials and mistakes he returns to his inherent dignity and finds his peace in you, his Maker.

To claim that all the human failures which frustrate love and understanding come only from your favorite children would be unfair to you, O Lord, and quite unjust to your creation. To see the one side of the coin and never look at the alternative is just as mean and narrow as to fret against the thunder, yet praise the fury of the flash which put the skies on fire.

We too have badly failed in our gift of love and to deny the share of our guilt would be sheer folly and presumption. What we have frequently presented to your friends as our token of affection was hardly worthy of its name. If it is true that our very nature seeks the joy of friendship and yearns to be a part of others, it is equally obvious that we are often tempted to be so selfish and conceited that no one else seems to exist in this small world of ours but our fortune and good luck. To put the famous sign of "NO-ADMITTANCE" on all the wings of our heart and grumble if we discover footsteps which do not honor our warning, this proves, O Lord, that between your friends and us is still the distance of two worlds. Not all of our privacy must vanish from the hours of our life — we need the stillness of our heart to let the harvest grow and ripen — but to exclude the next one from our love and care and treat him as if he never had a right to live, this is the deadly breeze which freezes all affections down to their very roots and makes US poorer than a beggar because WE lose the gracious aid our friends could offer to soothe our needs and deep afflictions. Although we know so clearly that we tire of the pleasures we take out from others yet never tire of those we give, our arrogance and pride continually seek to thrive at the expense of others, going as far as to be willing to secure their own existence by paying dearly for another's death: "Within us there is another evil in the same category of temptation, by which men are made vain though they do not please others or even displease others, and in any event have no desire to please others: but are interiorly pleased with themselves. They please themselves but mightily displease you." [5]

If a "closed" sign turns a heart into a desert, how much more a mind which flees from others and feeds on pride and prejudice. To judge by habit only from its own position and pronounce one's mind supreme destroys all reverence and love for the enormous differences in another human being. Tolerance supposes territories free of occupation, which minds conceited with their glory are never able to provide. To dictate is much easier than to inquire, to order more convenient than to ask. If tyranny rules long a nation, all other thoughts will perish soon, and with the death of mind our love will vanish, since men who oppress ideas quite readily oppress the human body. Arrogance blights all affections and reaps a harvest rich in tears. The tragic happenings of decades past not only provided a gruesome proof of this inevitable consequence, but also showed how God calls men to a terrible reckoning for his overweening pride: "Dearly they shall pay for their wandering from me, ruin follow on the heels of rebellion; I their ransomer and they so false! Never do their hearts cry out to me, growl they like beast in den." [6] May we never forget the horrendous lesson of the tragic past and prepare ourselves a little better for the uncertain future so that history has never to repeat those chapters which were the darkest our race has ever written.

Philosophers of old respected gods but saved their fondest admiration for the creature we call man. Of all the wonders they discovered, the greatest wonder was forever man. What makes a man a man, what ideas and dreams he cherished, why he was born and why he has to die — these questions challenged the wisdom of the ancients and spiraled their immortal epics to such excitable heights, that hardly anything which was written later could surpass their dynamic power or equal their intensity and drama. How do you

[5] Conf. 10. 39.
[6] Osee 7. 13–14.

wish to serve the gods, they asked, if you do not know how to serve men? Man's nature, even in its poor and frail mortality, was the highest print creation ever could have reached and man, as the recipient of this exciting glory, came close to reaching the powers of the gods. Without command he felt obliged to strive for pure perfection not only on the level of his body but much more in the disciplines of his skillful mind. A brilliant civilization, which inspired the human race with unheard of greatness and ambitions, accompanied this classic dream of man and left its indelible image even on the face of our century. To emulate with heroism and surpass any challenge, this was the only rivalry they knew and those who triumphed in this noble contest could count on everlasting fame and glory. By using all his talents to the limits could man discover real humanity? While straining all his skills could he unearth his inner self? To crown all fabulous achievements the ancients were aware of an eternal justice which they not only feared but tried to placate with their deeds of honor and of glory.

Yet one sentence was never mentioned in their brilliant message to all mankind, the sentence which we seek to memorize and try so hard to learn; "love the next one as you love yourself and do not hate your enemies." The ancients taught a universal view of man, that is true, but that was just as far as their minds could ever stretch. Love remained an unsung luxury, exchanged without great moment between secluded walls of families, yet not important enough to become the pillar of their whole religion. The key of their imagination, as brilliant as it was, never unlocked the chambers of the human heart nor did it release the mystery of love which once redeemed a world from its own disaster. Another had to come to bring the light which never fails.

Philosophers of our times lost their respect for God and saved for man DESPAIR. They took away from man the dignity and honor of being a masterpiece of heaven and leveled him ungracefully with the inhabitants of our jungles. It is from nature alone, they claim, that man has come into existence, in nature that he lives, and to nature that he returns when death subdues his booty. Man is a poor harried creature, whose essence is care, whose life is defeat, and whose end is death. The aimlessness of death is only the final seal on the aimlessness of life itself. Like an animal, man reflects only

23

the energies of nature, obedient only to her laws and plunged like the rest of matter, into a violent struggle for existence. In the end which is inevitable, man is bound to fail, since he is striving against insuperable odds and can not avoid being totally checked. The hero is not the man who sacrifices himself for others, but it is the man who fails bravely and genuinely, and genuine failure is a plunge into never ending darkness. Courage is demanded more than love. The best a man can do is to keep himself free for death since only by recognizing nothingness as his final end can man become a free and happy creature. Death makes the life that precedes death a meaningless answer to a meaningless question.

Such is the modern man of our enlightened century. After he was cruelly robbed of the dignity which God himself has bestowed on him, not much was left for man to make a man. Can such a man still love or bear the joy of being loved? Can he forget himself completely to think completely of the need and pains of others? Does he not see in others threats and dangers in his own struggle for survival? If man is only an animal with an animal faith, why should he not try to catch as much as he can in the way of animal enjoyment? To think of others in their need and even try to love them, more than himself, is purely a noble gesture which only they can easily afford who have enough to waste. Who will really consider me as a brother and not just as a label or a case in this world of "separate tables"? How can we establish a deep and meaningful personal relationship between beings which are not more than refined and well dressed animals? Can the heart survive in a depersonalized world, where big corporations rule supreme and request icy precision from man as well as tools? "We are all responsible for all." This was said so often by men of influence and stature that it has lost its hallowed power and turned into a glib slogan, used cunningly by demagogues who want to rule the world by violence and fear.

The modern man of our time is hardened and suspicious. He heard so much about the love of man but saw so little of it. More sermons will only do more harm. What he requests today is love itself and not a shiny counterfeit, presented in parades of clever promises or offered in exquisite speeches. Love is so noble an adventure that it shuns the multitude of declarations and seeks to hide behind the tender veil of sacrifices and of deeds. Chesterton said once: "The shadow of any momentary sparrow can be a message from the sun." Such a message might be little, its impact yet so great. The smile of any love can tell us that love still exists, and stirred up hope in darkness can reach and help despair. To awaken places in the heart of man which do not yet exist is of all discoveries perhaps the greatest we can make. Love alone can do it.

Men, in this age of unheard of riches, possess so much which they can spend and own so little with which they can truly live. For real love, pleasures are no longer necessary; yet if this real love has vanished from the altars of this world, pleasures can bring no joy but only greater hunger, which never can be stilled again but grows and grows until it dies: "Not death itself is so strong as love, not the grave itself cruel as love unrequited; the torch that lights it is a blaze of fire." [7]

Long ago a man, who was more than a man, brought down this blaze of fire into our midst and set the world on flames and we can surely assume these flames will continue to burn until the end of time. Our world will never grow so cold and gloomy that violence and greed will answer all the needs of man. In spite of our brutal wars and persecutions love will remain in our hearts and triumph at the very moment when our world is ready to surrender in despair. It was on the bloody hill of calvary, may we remember, where love struck its triumphant note of total victory: "All this I have told you, so that my joy may be yours, and the measure of your joy may be filled up. This is my commandment that you should love one another, as I have loved you. This is the greatest love a man can shew, that he should lay down his life for his friends; and you, if you do all that I command you, are my friends." [8]

[7] Cant. 8. 6.
[8] John 15. 11–13.

FOUR

The Song Of A Woman

The moral temperament of our people and the inner values they cherish and uphold are deeply influenced and decisively determined by the character and faith of our womanhood. The very level of the civilization which we so proudly call our own will rise and fall with the brilliant triumphs and shameful defeats of the best and worst of the representatives of our women. As long as they remain faithful to their chosen ideals and refuse violently to be degraded to the level of an interesting playtoy, our people will flourish and grow like a bountiful harvest under the rays of a benevolent sun; but if they choose to lower themselves and debase their innate dignity to please the demands of the highest bidder, all of us will suffer under a burning drought which easily might starve us to a slow and bitter death. All too often are the pages of history a powerful proof that the virtues of a woman have rallied imminent defeats into brilliant triumphs while great victories were often wrecked and spoiled because a woman's lust and vanity have dulled the edge of our swords.

Endowed with eternal beauty and alluring charm a woman radiates a glow of inner harmony and peace which easily stills the flow of quarrelsome blood and silences the age old cry of hatred and revenge.

Through the gentle expression of her inner riches and her many talents she imposes calm and serenity to the turbulent waves of distress and bitterness. Through the tender touch of her delicate hands, she heals so many wounds which man has caused with all his hateful wars and senseless persecutions. Gifted with boundless inner confidence and bestowed with enormous trust she lets her heart confide so easily and as long as her inner yearnings are not the target of deceit and trickery, she follows joyously the guiding light of her beloved destiny. Truly is said about her in the holy book: "Great content an industrious wife brings to her husband; health to every bone of his body is that good sense of hers. No better gift of God to man than a prudent woman that can hold her tongue; a soul well disciplined is beyond all price. Grace so gracious is none as woman's faithfulness and woman's modesty; woman's continence there is no valuing. Sun dawning in heaven can not match the lustre a good wife sheds on her home, and that beauty lasts into ripe age, like the glow of lights on the holy lamp-stand. Firm as golden pillar in silver socket rest the feet of steadfast woman on the ground she treads; and firm as foundations built for all time on solid rock is holy woman's loyalty to God's commandments." [1]

As the hungry soil on our teeming grounds waits for the fertile touch of our fiery spring, so yearns a woman in her bursting heart for the gentle embrace of man so that the cherished harvest — life — might begin to bloom in her golden tabernacle. In the exciting moments of fulfillment, when she is one in flesh with her beloved spouse, she approaches the threshold of a greatness which is only shared by the tremendous might of God himself. Chosen by the divine Wisdom and love to be a resting place of a new image of God's beauty and splendor, the woman carries a treasure under her heart which can never be bought or equalled by glittering gold or heavy silver. A savage only can entertain the coward thought of attacking or even destroying what heaven has presented to the woman as the most excellent gift on earth. To protect this tender life and feed these frail and helpless limbs until the child is vigorous enough to face the golden rays of our ardent sun, this is so sacred a duty that no one else is able and trained to fulfill it, but a mother alone. There can never be a substitute in this world for the selfless heart

[1] Ecclus. 26. 16–24.

27

of a humble mother. Poets might brilliantly write about the mysteries of life and compose artful hymns about its power and glory but it is up to the love of a woman to offer to us on our holy altars this precious and eternal gift. All the statues of fame wrestled away by the genius of man from a cold and clumsy stone remain frigid and lifeless while the woman, with her genial stroke of cooperation brings forth an exciting masterpiece which will live on forever. The greatest artist is not found amongst the poets or the writers; the greatest artist is forever our mother. Let us put the golden crown on her graceful forehead and we have made the best choice.

If man is more efficient and perhaps even more courageous in conquering the course of our fleeting hours, it will forever be the woman who rings a deeper echo for the call of eternity. Quickly disappointed with the calculated and brutal language of business and profits, she gladly fills her lips with melodies of love and mercy, ready to offer to us the vauable warmth of her affectionate heart. Not to hurt but to aid, not to deepen the dangerous abyss but to build a lofty bridge; these are the first and deepest instincts which the immortal soul of every woman offers to us in our greedy struggle for the dominion of our ever shrinking orbit. Less engrossed by the fabulous glitter of our technical marvels and mighty superstructures she keeps the best place in her heart free for the message from above. Heaven seems always a little closer to her longing heart than to the busy mind of the efficient man. Even in her way of thinking she expresses an affinity with the thoughts of heaven which is often surprising if not astonishing. Be it the unmarried daughter who surrenders herself completely to the services of her helpless mother or be it the tender wife who submits so gently to the growing demands of her beloved family or be it the blessed nun who refuses to share her beauty with anyone but God, we find in all of them, in different degrees perhaps, the footsteps of God who returns again to this turbulent world as a helpless beggar. As once before, the modern woman of today is willing to pronounce again the hallowed words: "BE it done unto me according to thy holy wish."

As long as a woman can give herself to the highest demands of God or to the needy mood of man, she enjoys a blessed tranquility of heart and a beautiful harmony of mind. Cursed is only the moment when she is not able to give or when the lively stream

28

of her giving is stalled by ridicule or marred by spite. Refused an outlet for the tremendous need of giving, she senses very soon a deeper feeling of frustration than a man because she had so much more in store to be spent on the heart of others. Like the beautiful season of spring which was never allowed to turn into the blessings of a long awaited summer, she returns the unspent enthusiasm of her waiting love into the narrow channels of her own disappointed heart where quickly an ominous wasteland begins to grow instead of a bounteous harvest.

Being so close to the imperceptible and slow growth of human life a woman perceives almost by necessity the precious art of waiting. The powerful wings of time are clipped and the impatient hours are flying slowly for her and almost every minute is counted by her shy and fearful lips. As the healthy seed in the warm and moisty furrow needs the helpful touch of all the various seasons to develop in vitality and exterior dimensions, so does a woman need her days and months to bring forth the crown of her harvest — the child —. Whoever tries to accelerate the time of this marvellous and mysterious process of the growth of human life will have to pay a stern and tragic price for such a folly. God is the author of human life as he is the maker of our body; He knows so well the moment which is the best to call us into existence, as he is so sure of the ways to perform this miraculous event. Let us be content to speed up our wheels and rudders but may we never touch the pointers of the clock of heaven.

This precious art of waiting — we might call it patience — is a deep source of inner valor and silent courage to a woman without which even a man could not endure the tensions and the perils of his inner life. He might not be aware of this fact as long as this beloved gift is near at hand and ready for his daily use, but if he loses it or if he prefers to throw it carelessly away, he begins to miss it more and more until he literally imperils the very balance of his weary mind. Not rarely has the sudden death of a beloved wife emptied entirely the meaning of life for her wailing husband. It does not seem to be the hardest stroke of fate if a broken heart is followed soon by a broken body. It might be true that a man is more vigorous and strong in the ever present hazard of a smaller storm which only shakes the edges of a fortress. He even might be able to endure more in the heat of our daily battles which are so much a part of our hourly diet, but comes the great crisis of life when everything is suddenly exposed to a shrieking, terrifying disaster, then it is the calm and serenity of a woman who tames the raging waves of the blinding storm and commands tranquility and peace again to the threatening might of the furious destruction. Amidst the ghostly ruins where the defeated man is tempted to surrender and to die, the woman is often courageous enough to withstand the eruption of agony and initiate again from an almost hopeless situation the greatest triumph on our history, the feast of resurrection.

In the powerful drama of Calvary where man tried so hard to destroy not only the life of our redeemer but also his hallowed memory, the woman proved to all of us that she possessed an intensity of faith in her courageous heart which is far greater than our feelings of fear and much stronger than all the ugly threats of persecution.

Who betrayed Christ? An apostle, who craved more for the glitter of money than for the exacting demands of honor and glory! When the decisive hour of history struck, when courage was needed more than anything else in this world, he found his shaky heart peddled away already for the possession of a tiny heap of moneypieces. So thoroughly blinded he was by the glow of riches that he did not even realize that he sold for so little what was worth so much.

Who surrendered Christ? A man in Roman armor, who had his rigid mind set on politics and his proud heart ruthlessly sold on personal triumphs and glories! With no great hesitation he twisted his curious mind and distorted the pages of the law to soothe the anger of his political opponents and silence their shouts for bloody revenge.

Where were the apostles in this hour of need? Trembling behind locked doors in fear of the Jews!

There still was the strongman Peter, who was called the rock; where was he? In front of a female attendant he swore repeatedly that he had never met Christ.

One man only had the inner fortitude to face the final disaster of Christ on the Cross; John, the apostle, to whom our helpless Lord confided the safety and care of his own beloved mother.

Who proclaimed Christ's innocence in that tumultuous hour when everyone shouted for the crucifixion of Christ? A Roman matron, the governor's wife, whose name was Claudia. She implored her husband to have nothing to do with that just man, for she had suffered many things on that day on account of him.

Who showed sympathy with our Lord when he dragged himself forward on his bloody road to the distant hill? The pious women of Jerusalem with their children in their arms, ignoring the mockery of the rabble and consoling our Master with their mournful tears. How gladly Christ must have stopped to look at them and to say: "It is not for me that you should weep, daughters of Jerusalem; you should weep for yourselves and your children. Behold a time is coming when men will say, it is well for the barren, for the wombs that never bore children and for the breasts that never suckled them. It is then that they will begin to say to the mountains, fall on us and to the hills, cover us. If it goes so hard with the tree that is still green, what will become of the tree that is already dried up?" [2]

Later on it was Veronica who imposed courageously a hold to this caravan of death and stretched forth the linen cloth so that our Lord could wipe away the bloody dust from his weary face.

Who was with Christ when the peak of the hill was finally reached and who remained there until lightning flashed from the angry sky and tore apart the veil of the temple? Mary, his mother, and Cleophas, the sister of Mary and Mary Magdalene, the woman who was a sinner. They had taken their stand beside the cross of Jesus and they professed with their very presence to the Roman soldiers and to the Jewish leaders that they loved Christ till the tragic end.

Not one woman can be named or singled out who fled from Christ or abandoned him in his hour of death. Not one woman can be cited who has betrayed God in the forum of public opinion or has denied that she knew her beloved Master. All of them remained faithful to their belief, and they refused to yield their loyalty to threats of persecution. No wonder that God had loved them so much that he chose one of them to be his blessed Mother. Ave Maria. Hail to you Mary.

The woman of today has made mistakes, no doubt, and she will continue to inscribe failures into the pages of her daily accounts. Possessing so great a potential of emotions and feelings she might easily be tempted to stress the powers of her heart too much and act too often against the better warnings of her worried mind. Perturbed by

[2] Luke 23. 28–31.

her aroused sentiments and agitated by her disturbed affections she might fully disregard the signals of her intellect and make decisions which she later on regrets so deeply. "Why did I do that" is not the rarest question of a woman in distress. Many an unfortunate incident could have been avoided and numerous tragic moments would never have occurred if the woman had offered to her troubled mind a greater chance to express itself and if she had hearkened more readily to her better judgment. Sufferings and hurts which were created by the overstressed preponderance of the emotions would never have entered her life had she better preserved the precarious balance between mind and heart. Jealousy, the stinging poison of her joys and laughter, would never have taken so strong a grip on her very life, had she followed more rigidly the warnings of her intellect and reason.

In her quest for more rights the woman might easily be misguided and tempted to go too far in her demands. Dreaming about a fairyland of freedoms she might not rest until she has achieved perfect equality with man, forgetting that perfectly equal never means perfectly happy. Being endowed by God with entirely different talents and skills, she has a varied mission to fulfill in this world, and she would only sacrifice all the outstanding features of her lovely being and turn into a bleak shadow of her own self if she presses her demands for emancipation too rigidly and carries her quest to the extremes. To rival man on his own terms could turn out to be the greatest error the modern woman has committed in our times. This error could heap disgrace and destruction on the very roots of her existence. At best she would only become a poor imitation of an ideal which is completely foreign to her mission and hurtful to her deepest aspirations and desires. Will not all of us suffer and register a bitter failure in our lives if the woman of today strives to become more and more like a man and forgets that all we want and need in this troubled world is more and more of a pure and faithful woman? As a flower is not really free if we cut it away from its very roots and praise it as liberated, so can a woman never claim inner freedom and perfect happiness if she loses the very soil of her inner growth and development and changes into the cold climate of another human being. I am afraid that if the woman ever reaches perfect equality with man, she would suddenly feel frustrated and disillusioned and quite a few would turn out to be bored, sarcastic and at the end immoral.

Real love never seeks its own self as it strives by its very nature to be given to someone else. To love oneself is a bitter illusion. When the real function of love is misinterpreted by a woman or misunderstood, she defies her own purpose and creates a twofold danger; she cheapens her love to a vile and easy object of greed and lust or she withdraws her tender gift from the lips of others and withers away unwanted and never desired. If however the enthusiasm of her heart is well disciplined and kindly guided by mature and selfless reason, she will always be a blessing and a ray of sunshine in the midst of a hopeless winter.

Long ago I heard a marvelous legend which I liked so much that I still remember it so vividly as if one had narrated it to me only yesterday. In a gilded castle on a rather high mountain lived once a beautiful lady who was so splendorous in her appearance that no one could ever enjoy her presence without admiring and praising her fascinating beauty. At first the noble lady was not perturbed by all this rapt attention and open flattery since she was good of heart and of a very gentle mind. All too soon however she realized, to her own great disappointment, that vanity took more and more of her attention especially at the moments when she gazed joyously at the soft and delicate features of her graceful hands. Not willing to endure much longer these sweet and tempting thoughts, she firmly and swiftly decided to hide forever the lovely features of her spotless hands under the dark cover of a pair of silken gloves. No sooner did she put on this tender armor of protection than she felt that the power of vanity lost its grip on her soul and deep calm commenced again to reign in her exalted heart.

Winter came. With its bleak and hardened fingers it seized the frozen land and covered with the heavy flakes of snow the roofs of all the cities. Was there anyone who would dare to tread upon this white and icy carpet which looked so gentle and so innocent and yet was ever treacherous and faithless? Yes, there was one. An old woman, bent by years and sorrows, defied the bitter cold and stepped ahead through the deep snow hoping and praying that she reach in time the stately gates of the gilded castle. At last she arrived. With a deep sigh of relief, she knocked at the heavy portals and soon found the entrance open. The glorious lady of the house was waiting. Silently they faced each other and no one counted the moments which passed so slowly as never before in their different lives. Suddenly the beautiful lady took off her dark and silken gloves and put them gently but firmly on the frozen hands of the abandoned woman. For the first time in many years she saw her own hands bare again. With a triumphant surprise she could gaze at them, enjoy their tender features, and praise God for their precious beauty without the slightest pride or vanity. By helping another woman she had conquered herself. So far the legend.

The modern woman of today is not called upon to give up loving; she is asked by all of us to begin to love truly. Only with this rare gift of true love will she be strong enough to help us to find those everlasting values which give our troubled life a deeper meaning. Only with this true love is she holy enough to lead man back again to the waiting heart of God.

FIVE

Pointers On My Crossroads

To the delight of old and young we are setting out today on a long and beautiful journey from which perhaps we will never return. With all our preparations cleared, we await eagerly the announcement of our destination. Are we going to scale the wild peak of a majestic mountain where we could so easily snatch away the favorite rays of the golden sun? Or are we reaching for the charming shore of the ocean where the greedy floods pitch so furiously against the helpless sand while we stand so firmly entrenched amidst the arrogant waves testing the courage of our body and of our mind? Or are we ambitious enough to discover and explore the boundaries of a mysterious kingdom, hidden somewhere in a far distant corner of an obscure stretch of land upon which no conqueror has ever laid his sword? Yes, to all these beautiful sites we will journey and our voyage will take in all these marvelous views and still there will be more, much more to be revealed to us. From the beckoning heights of the mountains and the turbulent shore of the sea, from the boundaries of all the kingdoms we will move on and on, farther and farther to the distant horizon until we reach the long desired, final point of our pilgrimage — infinity.

This infinity is set before our eyes as the ultimate aim of our trip and no one amongst us, rich or destitute, can ever afford to miss it. Those who fail have betrayed their very life. How can we make sure that we find the right direction? How can we avoid going astray in our search for our final triumph?

Three pointers are given to us to guide us along on our lonely and often dangerous road and each of these pointers carries a request which God himself has written so wisely on all the different signposts. These requests must be fulfilled by every pilgrim before he is allowed to call his journey completed.

More curious than serious we hastily approach the first pointer and we find there the written command — DO NOT JUDGE. Reading it leisurely we do not register at first any perturbance in our hardened mind, but after some serious reflection this request begins to press harder and harder on our awakening conscience and almost suddenly we question ourselves, "Am I the person who is warned? Do I possess the dubious distinction of judging others without any reason or without any right? Have I, with my subtle insinuations or with the crude outburst of my poor temper, destroyed the precious peace of others? Or was I suave enough to hide my real intentions and keep the judgment in my mind where God can read it like an open book? Is it not true that the tendency to judge is in all of us? Do not all of us feel a little better the moment we criticize the mind of another?"

Those amongst us who are very proud often have to hide many things which are wrong. Unable to tame our own inner unrest, we project our discontent into the life of others and utter so swiftly our hardened suspicions instead of lavishing generous praise. A few amongst us, frustrated perhaps by our own bitter dreams, grow so harsh and distrustful that we never allow again greatness to enter our bleak and lonely existence. Not able to reach the peak of the mountains ourselves, the mountain has to shrink to our own ridiculous size to satiate pitiful hunger. Only if everything shrinks will a petty heart find rest.

To a man who judges others severely we should submit the simple question — "Friend, what bothers you in your heart?" If I can not perceive any good in the life of another, how can I enjoy the good in myself? It is like keeping the sun out of my heart and shutting tightly the windows of my soul. I just beg darkness to be the only light which I can follow in my dreary walk through life. A Christian saint said once: "When you perceive in your brother anything worthy of reprehension, turn your eyes upon yourself. Before you judge him examine yourself well and if you find that you are guilty of the same fault, pronounce the sentence against yourself saying with the prophet — "It is I. I am he who sinned, I have done wickedly."

But there must be some situations, you may object, where I can afford the luxury of judging others. After all, I do not mean to harm the character of my friend; I just utter my judgment to alleviate my own inner pressure. Can there be any wrong involved in such a judgment? Let us borrow the answer to this question from St. Paul who writes: "wherefore thou art inexcusable, oh man, who ever thou art, who judgest, for wherein thou judgest another thou dost condemn thyself for thou who judgest dost the same thing thyself."

More serious than curious we walk ahead now eager to learn the request which is written on the second signpost and there we find one word only — FORGIVE.

To forgive is an art which everyone has to learn but in which only few excel. No one is however excused from trying. We may have an excuse for not being a genius or a dramatic poet, but who can ever find an excuse for not forgiving? Each one of us has to take this divine request to his own heart, build it into his own life and make it the pillar of his whole inner worth. Each one of us with no particular exception. Only the idiot, who can not distinguish between good and evil, is freed from this great obligation.

We have to forgive everyone. The names of my friends and of my enemies are on my daily list and not rarely do we find it harder to forgive a friend than an enemy. Why this strange repugnance? Why can we be so slow to forgive a friend who has offended us? If we love someone we are forever tempted to read his name — heaven — and we forget so easily the other word which is spelled — dust. Our demands towards the beloved become exorbitant and at certain times almost unreasonable. We are trying too hard and too selfishly to claim from a friend a manifestation which we have no right to demand nor the privilege to enjoy. After all, only God can claim infinite goodness and beauty. My friend, even my best friend, labors under his limitations and suffers under his failures. So

37

let us be humble in our demands and conciliatory with our friends, satisfied with simply having them, not entering their feelings nor begging for their secrets, but really content to be able to walk together through this fascinating world of ours. Let us never forget that our friends are made to the image of God and not to the fiction of our fickle fancy.

Often the younger ones find it harder to bend their heart to forgiveness than those whose hair has been whitened by the burden of their many years. Is it perhaps that the young man is so sure that he can conquer everything? Are not fences for him a sign which has to be broken down? Why study the gracious art of losing if one can memorize so well the way to win? Patience and understanding are relics only of years gone by, beautiful and venerable without doubt, but with no message left for our modern era. If such a youth is struck deeply with the bitter sting of an offense he has no way to reply. Stung beyond comprehension, he endures the hated insult like a deadly blow which is much stronger than his very pulse of life. Many a tragedy was written in such a fatal moment and the life of a few has ended where it just should have begun to bloom.

The man who is unselfish in his ways of life will always be most gracious in forgiving. Hate can only survive in a heart which has ceased to give. A heart like that circulates red blood only, warming a body which has died before his own death. May this unhappy man with his cursed existence never carry my own name. Forgiveness was the sublimest petition which Christ had uttered from his bloody pulpit. No other command was so beautiful as no other command was so hard. The strong ones who are willing to try it perceive how difficult it can be while the weakling with his flippant lips declares it smilingly, "a virtue for the cowards." To all of us however, weak or powerful, hateful or loving, our Lord has said, "Your heavenly Father will forgive you your transgressions if you forgive your fellow-men theirs; if you do not forgive them, your heavenly Father will not forgive your transgressions either."

Deeply serious and with greater caution we move ahead trying to reach the last signpost before our journey will find its end. Here we face the shortest request of all — GIVE. This seems to be easy and with a deep sigh of inner relief, we hastily begin to count the total number of our generous triumphs. Yet before we indulge too seriously in our wide and multicolored show of magnanimity, let us ask the simple question — "Have I really given?" Was not my so-called gift a pure token of a perfect exchange? Surely I gave but only because I expected something in return. Such a gift does not deserve its name since possessions changed only their place with no one gaining anything from any one else. Such a social transaction creates no echo in the heavens above as nothing is really left which can be rewarded by God. But, you may object swiftly, your generous gift was far more than a pure exchange; it was a significant contribution which exercised a tremendous effect on the development of your school, the growth of your parish and perhaps even on the welfare of your own beloved city. You even remembered the numerous telegrams, beautiful flowers and most sincere congratulations which poured so enthusiastically into your besieged office to let you know how pleased everyone seems to be with the generous gesture of your rich and bounteous heart. Your name was even painted in ornamented letters on the very first page of your local paper so that everyone who could master the script knew that you were the undisputed hero. "Mercedem vani receperunt — They have received the reward of the vain." Why should Our Lord remunerate us for something which was not done for Him but for our own tiny glory?

Behind my gift must be my very heart and not my cool and clever calculation. If my heart carries my present, then even the mite of the widow will bring pure joy to God the Almighty, but if this heart of mine is missing, even gold and silver will be cheaper than a heap of dust.

No one can refrain from giving. As there is no man who can inhale only, so is there no man in our midst who can only take. We have to give not only from our intelligence and wisdom which can broaden so far the horizons of man, but also from our material affluence with which God has blessed us so astonishingly to let a begging friend or a hated enemy starve to the shape of a skeleton or freeze to a premature and useless death — this is a grave responsibility which not a single member of our human family can easily shrug off or escape by pretending "not to know." Today we count too many men in our midst whose possessions are so bountiful but whose heart has grown so hopelessly small. Greed became the undisputed and ugly dictator of so many an account in our fire-proof

39

money safes. To invest more and more means so often to give less and less until we reach the fatal moment when we are devoured by our own rapacious hunger. A miser can never be thrilled by his laughter since he is always haunted by the frightful echo of the penny spent. He jails his own joys and offers to the begging lips a kiss which is not only cold but frozen. Real greatness will always shun the man who is haunted by the burning ambition of gathering more and more, while his thirsting heart remains so pitifully empty.

The greatest hour in our life is still ahead of us. In a few years perhaps — or sooner — the most important meeting in my life will take place and will decide my eternal future. God the great one and I the little one will face each other and no one knows of course whether this terrifying meeting will turn into a blessing or into bitter curse. One thing we are sure of is that we can make these tremendous moments earlier, if not friendlier, if we can say to our Lord and Master, "Look, whatever you have entrusted to my solicitude and care I have spent amongst those who needed it more than I. Even my very life I surrendered so that another could live."

Gradually the tired sun is setting behind the majestic peaks of those distant mountains which shroud, like a tender veil, the mysterious land of infinity. Our beautiful journey approaches slowly its last minutes. One last question lingers on the mind of all of us, "Was our voyage a success or a bitter failure?" Soon the answer will be given to us but only if we passed victoriously the three different signposts, if we harkened to the various requests of God and tried, time and again, not to judge, to forgive and to give. Then we are justified to cherish the hope — the jubilant hope — that our next step will be a triumphant step into the eternal bliss of heaven.

SIX

There Are My Ambitions

Ambitions are magic. For the stream of life they are exactly what the current is for our rivers. Their dynamic strength not only propels our mind to climb to unexpected heights but generates also powers which can light up the corners of the universe and even change the face of our earth. Ambitions bring out the best in man or the worst, like the rapacious current of an excited sea which is at times wild and destructive, at other times a prayer for blessing in a land of drought and sorrow. Good or evil, ambitions are needed and the man who is without their fire reminds us so much of a corpse which somehow still manages to move.

We hate to be failures. Planted deeply in the open furrows of our heart is the precious seed of success and no one should ever seriously attempt to destroy this precious offering which was so carefully sowed by the loving hands of our Lord. To wish to become a success is not enough. We need the iron determination to follow our star and never to rest until the crown is ours. Some of us remain in the "wishing-state" until we depart from the streets of this world, leaving behind a memory which is as empty as our life was, while others are determined to put the highest price on their ambitions, knowing that ambitions are the elements which make our life worth living. If a man has realized his longings and sees his aspirations prosper, he is not afraid of his last hours. Death is for him not a hated or a futile dream but the beginning of a life which will last forever. Ten talents he received from his Lord and Master and with twenty talents he returns to his Redeemer to give an account of his faithful stewardship.

Ambitions reflect different colors. They mean different things to different men. What they however request from all of us is hard and disciplined work. Without this work our ambitions are destined to die the minute they should commence to live. If we are willing, however, to exert ourselves for the success of our aspirations and concentrate our energies on a bold and daring challenge, success and fame will lend their taste to our lips. Not that the smiles of fortune are the highest goals of our virtues — they never will be more than the shadows to the sun — but they spur us on not only to appear the best but to be the best. In this shallow age of ours where the glitter of the toys darkens so much the real and everlasting values, we are in desperate need of men and women who value character and truth more than cheap and gaudy notoriety. There is no real and enduring satisfaction in being praised for something small or transitory nor is there lasting joy in being applauded for deeds which others performed for our name; it must be the harvest of our own labors which will bring peace and satisfaction to our restless souls.

Healthy ambitions are not greedy for conquest nor do they strive for power and might. The man who deserves to be the leader is not running after the crown but has to be found by those who are eager and willing to put the precious insignia on his humble forehead. If one however offers himself as a ruler or heralds his talents on the public square, let us watch him carefully for many seasons, lest we offer our laurels to a bloody tyrant or expose our trust to the whims of a clown. People who are over-eagerly ambitious are more of a menacing threat to us than a petitioned blessing. Full of themselves they set aside the hours of the night for the dreams of their own making and all the hours of the day are used for the increase of their own glory and deceit. If they spell a name correctly, it surely must be their own. As history proves it so often, there is more harm done to a nation by the vanity of ambitions than by a sword which is too sharp. The best cure perhaps for aspirations grown too high and spread too thin is a sound and thorough defeat. Should history not provide this golden medicine, God certainly will do it. The tragic end of many dictators and self-styled rulers could have been avoided had these tyrants learned to tame their destructive avalanche of vain ambitions: "The disciples came to Jesus at this time and said, Tell us who is the greatest in the Kingdom of heaven? Whereupon Jesus called to his side a little child, to whom he gave a place in the midst of them and said, Believe me, unless you become like little children again, you shall not enter the kingdom of heaven. He is greatest in the kingdom of heaven who will abase himself like this little child." [1]

Since nothing has never created anything, a clumsy sluggard will often complain about the apparent lack of inviting opportunities. Forever WAITING for the happy stroke of luck the bells refuse to toll his sunshine. The great chance of our lifetime will gently offer itself in direct proportion to our ability and our determined will for action and inversely escape our reach and our attention in proportion to our sloth and cowardice.

In recent years a trend has developed in our national climate, which has to be deeply regretted and deplored, the raving passion, if not obsession, to imitate others. Our mass production on the gray and boring assemblyline has not only constructed machines of the same type and value but it has also fabricated men of the same pattern and equal standards. Our flattened mirrors reflect always the same faces although different people look into the glass at various times. We are inclined to think like others, dress like others, build our roofs like others and to make it still more obvious talk and laugh like all the others. To step away from the fences of the herd is regarded as a temptation and should one try too hard to outwit the wisdom of the assemblyline he is considered strange or even dangerous. To fight and suffer alone, if necessary, for the power of an idea or bring sacrifices for one's conviction, this has become a rarity in our times which only few in our midst enjoy. More and more become reluctant to follow a course which is not popular although they are deeply convinced in the better part of their timid souls that this would be the only course which is just and right. To hide a

[1] Matt. 18. 1–4.

frustrated conscience behind the silly rules of "play-it-safe" and bequeath all heroism to the blessed saints and martyrs, this is the smart and ONLY way to play the game and pluck the harvest of success. Prosperity at any price, this is the greatest vow they ever pronounce and if moral values stand against their greed and profits, they have no choice but to capitulate. Whatever could spoil or menace their bloody harvest better disappears from our silent heavens and from our numbed and tired consciences.

The real quality of our ambitions is measured by its intensity rather than by its heights. Our will has to exert its might in our aspiration not only our emotions or our feelings. "To find a solution to this problem or to provide one" this is the best title which should caption all the pages of our life. Being strong in our will and firm in our determination does not always imply to speak with a loud voice or flex our tensed up muscles — these manifestations could easily hide a coward — but it means to make our dreams come to LIFE. To dream at times is good since an occasional dream is an invigorating and often an inspiring experience as long as we realize that we have to return again from our dream land to this valley of tears to fulfill our obligations and to pay our bills. Mere resolutions, however, without a strong determination in their wings, slow down the path of our best ambitions and paralyze our drives to a standstill. Our prizes and our crowns are not bestowed on music which was nicely written yet was never played, nor are we thrilled by great inventions which looked so fine on paper but never could be realized. Deeds are expected and admired, deeds which prove that a man has reached maturity and strength. Even in our holy faith dreams and wishes alone do not secure our final bliss in heaven: "Of what use is it, my brethren, if a man claims to have faith, and has no deeds to shew for it? Can faith save him then? Here is a brother, here is a sister, going naked, left without the means to secure their daily food; if one of you says to them, Go in peace, warm yourselves and take your fill, without providing for their bodily needs, of what use is it? Thus faith, if it has no deeds to shew for itself, has lost its own principle of life." [2]

A rather critical situation sets into our life the very moment we like to believe that we have finally learned enough and that our

[2] James 2. 14–17.

knowledge has climbed a peak from where there is no further as-
cent. Possessing all the solutions and replies we feel so secure that we
fail to recognize our own limitations and inadequacies. Completely
disregarding all the necessary cautions, we commence to utter opinions and statements when prudent silence would have saved us much
embarrassment and shame. The mature person, however, who is
only too convinced of his shortcomings and failures looks upon
learning as a perpetual source of joy and satisfaction. To close the
book at the end of a calendar or terminate the thrill of new discoveries at the stroke of an hour is next to impossible for such a
humble and creative mind. Not that we imply that the pages of a book
contain all the wisdom we need — experience must never be forgotten — but the solid study of the printed word sharpens the mind
and enlarges our horizon. Many new continents of knowledge wait for
its revelation and various question marks expect to be erased. Are we
then allowed to let dust settle on our intellect and give to leisure
the greater part of our energies?

The knowledge gained should always be less of a comfort than
the mysteries which wait to be discovered. Old customs and anti-
quated answers are disintegrating around us like castles built on
sand and the rising tide of new sciences about the space above and the
sea below are fascinating anew the power of our mind and the discipline of our intellect. We need not be philosophers who try to find
the last replies to our many questions but searchers and inven-
tors who gently contribute their own inconspicuous share to the ultimate conquest of the universe. Alone we never suffice to master this
tremendous challenge. By far the greatest part of our knowledge
on which we base the fundamentals of life will flow from the experience of others. Other minds, wiser perhaps than we or equally
foolish, have labored for the solutions of our problems hundreds
of years ago, as we perhaps, wittingly or unwittingly open up avenues which only future generations are blessed to enjoy. After searching for our abilities first, we should clasp the hand of our friends and
accept the help they offer us. Willingness to seek and accept advice
is one of the outstanding characteristics of a great and learned
man.

It is in the nature of studies that errors are made. Every ambition, as illustrious as it might be, must expect to encounter fail-

45

ures. Difficulties, not the mirror, show us of what we are really made. Great mistakes and small ones are the stepping stones on which we climb to the triumphant peak of truth. Without failures we would still roam around in the darkness of the stone age with the dense jungle as the roof to our homes. A few consider failures as something negative which has to be regretted like any other nuisance which wastes our time and drains our energies. Yet they may overlook the fact that the very failure we decry has cleared the path for the mind of the inventor and propelled his thoughts into the right direction to the final triumph. The only way to cope with failures is to expect our proper share and to refuse to be chained by our errors into sloth and bitterness. A coward is always a sorry sight on the battlefield as well as in the laboratory. Soon he will find so many things impossible or too risky whereas the courageous thinker continues in his analysis of problems, calculates his chances and is rewarded at the end with the thrill of success. Not that we invite anyone to disregard the presence of menacing cliffs and threatening avalanches; this would be foolish and could lead into a disaster, but to be more afraid of the danger than to be prepared to meet it, this is the sign of a coward.

Mentally and physically we develop at different rates of speed. No time schedule can ever be fixed which determines every detail of our growth and expansion. Some in our midst bloom late while others are ready to sprint with the golden rays of the rising sun. Early or late remains however irrelevant as long as we are firmly determined to advance with the passing of the years and not to turn into a muddy pool of stagnant waters. As long as this precious ability to think grows and sharpens and as long as our inner riches and experiences multiply, we have not lost anything even if we started late to conquer.

Growing ambitions bring increased success and power and it is the benevolent use of power on which our happiness and peace are founded. If our ambitions are accompanied by a right and humble heart, we will never seek success at the expense of others; but if greed is the only root of our drives and passions, we will not hesitate to employ brutality and revenge just to secure a more prolific profit. To enjoy the bliss of life at the expense of another one's death is such a repulsive idea that only few are able to entertain it in their twisted mind. May it be false to state that their hideous number is growing in our precarious times.

To remain modest through all our soaring triumphs and costly defeats is an art which all of us have to learn but in which only few excel. Conceit and pride are the stigmas of a fool. As little brooks are often noisier than mighty seas and oceans, cheap ambitions are more turbulent and clamorous than the noble and the great ones. Those who are vain enough to whine and beg for another round of loud applause may only harvest ridicule. The great ones in our midst who only feel that they performed their duty will easily receive our hearts and our praises. Perhaps the warning of St. Paul, as old as it might sound, has still a decisive meaning for our age which claims to be so far advanced and skillful: "After all, friend, who is it that gives thee this pre-eminence? What powers hast thou, that did not come to thee by gift? And if they came to thee by gift, why dost thou boast of them, as if there were no gift in question?" [3]

Fearful prophets like to tell us that we are living in a time of unprecedented crisis and that we should brace ourselves to meet the worst. Measured by the tranquility and calm which pervaded the climate of previous centuries, their statement might contain some truth, but if we gauge our era according to the challenges it offers, then it is one of the most blessed of all centuries. Dangers certainly surround us as greedy vultures surround a fighting tiger, but these dangers are fraught with opportunities which we can find or lose. The man of magnificent ambitions is alert enough to face the threats of the danger and at the same time brilliant enough to seize the opportunities. As no other man in our midst he is gifted to be the leader of the future.

[3] I Cor. 4. 7.

SEVEN

Who Shares My Failures

Man, in the raw, is a forceful blend of ruthless contradictions which stubbornly defy attempts of harmony and reconciliation. Entangled in some fearful tensions which heaven and earth stir up in his coveted soul, man has to endure the brunt of bitter conflicts that in return adorn his heart with magnificent achievements or shame his mind with violent defeats.

As the mystery of the human soul is never covered with one single line, so is the life of man never fully analyzed as a complete success or as a total failure. Whether we like it or not, our existence is a mixture of the two and the more mature we are, the easier we recognize the lines of demarcation. Success builds well on failure and balances it carefully just as the golden rays of our sun stimulate and proportion the intensity and range of the inevitable shadow.

Of these two guests who constantly invite themselves to our table and stay with us as long as we deserve, we first consider failures because they are harder to accept and more painful to endure than sheer prosperity and joy.

Failures are a test of man, permitted by God in order to diminish the allurements of this present world and to augment, in the same proportions, the attractions of the eternal life. Better than any other examen do failures expose the inner capacities of man and reveal the worth of promises he made. When we have need of being cleansed and deepened so as to collaborate with God in the salvation of this world, God strikes the soul as hard as he struck Saul when he was on his way to persecute the Christians in the city of Damascus. We might perhaps find happiness without the failures of our life, but one would never be aware of such a happiness unless one rescued it with danger from the abyss of its complete extinction.

Failures can become so wide a land in man's allotted province that some of us are just not able any more to cross this arid stretch of land without the painful feelings of discouragement and without the sting of bitter disappointments. Sad and disillusioned, we ask ourselves whether it is not useless to begin again if so many beginnings turned only into cruel endings. Why be disheartened anew if it can be avoided at the price of final resignation?

Failures have a way to penetrate deeply into the furrows of our heart leaving behind their scars which often never disappear again from our dreams of life until this life itself is totally exhausted or spent in remorse and despair. Like a destructive undercurrent, past failures can persistently flow through the endeavors of our mind and lame, with spiteful memories, the stream of brighter dreams.

The bitterest taste of failure consists not in the failure itself but in the train of endless thoughts and questions which they raise in our harassed mind and in our troubled judgment. Instinctively we always claim that with some better care or brighter luck a failure could have been avoided. We forget so easily that it was God who wrote this hurting letter and that it was He who put this letter in the mail. The moment we see in errors and defeats only the reverse side of God's eternal love and mercy, this very moment our heavy burden becomes acceptable to our mind and for some perhaps lighter to carry.

The responsibility of deciding involves quite often a risk of going astray and such a risk belongs to the essence of making decisions. Going astray however carries some sort of punishment which seems to follow swiftly, and this kind of penalty and trial belongs to the substance of failures. No wonder that so many of us, with hardly an exception, have paid reluctant tribute to this alliance of distress and that we suffered deeply under the harsh lesson which failures have taught their many students in this world. Limited as we are in our intellectual grasp of situations and poorly advised at times in the choice of actions against expected gains, we step so often into chains of disappointments in which we anticipated wings of freedom and success. We failed, no doubt, and we will fail in many enterprises of the future; yet failures will never strike us as a matter of surprise but more as fact of logical conclusion. Would we not be amazed if man, with partial knowledge and curtailed experience, would never make decisions which he regrets because they were so utterly incompetent and foolish? He failed, we are apt to say, because he was just human. A perfect record is not the destiny of man. But if we hear that Christ has failed, he who was so gifted to be a great success, we find it hard to understand and even harder to believe. Yet our Lord met this bitter rival of success not only once but often; he encountered failures and defeats when we expected him to harvest triumphs and success.

Born as a leader, Christ possessed all the necessary talents to make his superb mission on earth a conquest without end. HE commanded the power of speech in a degree rarely found in other rulers of his time. He knew also how to use it to perfection. Only a forceful orator of exceptional quality was mighty and persuasive enough to keep huge crowds listening for hours and to make them forget what they usually never forget, that they were hungry and exhausted. His enemies, always present in his audience, attested unwillingly to his superb delivery and fascinating style when they reported to the cunning Pharisees: "Nobody has ever spoken as this man speaks."

As a leader, Christ could not afford to let a dark spot settle on the garment of his holy mission nor could suspicions be allowed to creep into his glorious message of redemption. The Heavens had to be immaculate and no cloud was permitted to hide the splendor of his majestic life. So he could say in confidence and truth what other leaders never dared to mention: "Can anyone of you convict me of sin?"

A leader has to look attractive. People who listen usually watch. Not only the message excites their interest but also the man who delivers it. As far as the bodily form and physical features of Christ are concerned, we are dependent on pure conjecture. This is more evident from the marvelous variety of pictures and representations which artists of all centuries have conceived to portray their greatest inspiration. Although none of them can claim to have achieved a total likeness, everyone perhaps succeeded in bringing back again into reality some aspects of the majesty of their model. Relying on the Old Testament passage which describes the conquering King-Messias as: "Thine is more than mortal beauty, thy lips overflow with gracious utterance," we might well assume that our Lord possessed an overwhelmingly impressive personality giving his human appearance a dignity and charm which have endured already two thousand years and have not lost their luster.

In spite of all these outstanding characteristics of leadership and inspiration, in spite of three years of excessive labor and of preaching, Christ could never conquer the stubborn heart of his own people, which he loved so much but which received him not: "For ever his brethren were without faith in him."

Like any other people, the Jews were full of life, highly impressionable and quickly moving. Deeply responsive if something new began to glitter on their small horizon, they became very excited if sensational happenings were in the secret offerings. Inflamed quite readily with the enthusiasm of new hopes and glories, they swiftly changed applause to anger when fear or hatred imposed on their alarming cries a different direction.

Deep under the influence of the moment, the Jewish crowds like any other crowd in history could hardly follow their way straight and orderly, as they were always secretly afraid to find themselves, at last, with no place left to hide or flee. Whoever was the first and loudest in his appeal to their enormous vanity and pride had surely the greatest chance to gain the smile of their approval.

In every massive throng there is an ugly streak of violence which can not be defined by reason. Emotional in its birth and emotional in its death, such violence is far beyond the reach of explanation and has to be endured as we endure a blessing or a curse. In its effects it can be smooth, like well tamed animals, or reckless like ferocious beasts. "Hosanna to the king of kings" and "to the cross with him," these shouts of joy and hatred were easily combined and reconciled by hearts who had no share or interest in either.

A multitude will never be a showplace for the spirit. Crowds are not fascinated by ideas but by their trimmings. For learned sermons there is but little use; yet, for parades with miracles and shows, they have a vast room in their simple hearts. How easily they are thrilled by glitter and by pomp almost like children glowing over shiny toys.

Christ's personality had strong, intellectual undertones; one had to think to understand his message. If one failed to develop an inner sense of beauty and of grandeur or never yearned for all the splendor of eternal happiness, the promises of our Lord lost their appeal. If one could never fathom the greatness of the sermon on the mount, Christ had nothing to offer but dreams and dreams are the one commodity for which a crowd just has no use. They had to keep their fingers in the wily scramble for their daily bread; they had to run and run to gain some good positions in this brutal race for better and for more. What had no message for their stomach surely had no message for their mind. No wonder that "they understood him not," especially not in that precarious moment when the delicate situation grew serious and assumed a danger which hardly anyone had wished to face.

Who wants to contradict the mighty opinion of a political party which distributes the wealth of the land?

Who desires to show his courage and his determination at the expense of losing favor with the ruling cast?

Why dare to alienate the golden feelings for good business which in return might well secure prosperity and even offer some attractive jobs?

Who wants to hear of sacrifices and of death?

Play it safely and condemn Christ as a criminal. The shortest way to lose so little and the best way to gain so much! Anyhow, something must be true about the rumors they spread about the life of Christ; otherwise this man from Nazareth would be defended by the law and surely set free by justice. But everyone seems to be convinced that he is guilty, and if everyone is convinced about his guilt, how can it be different? Can Christ be right if so many believe that he is wrong? Get rid of him, destroy his memory, and let the painful incident be totally forgotten.

Christ, however, could not forget: "Jerusalem, Jerusalem, still murdering the prophets, and stoning the messengers that are sent to thee, how often have I been ready to gather thy children together, as a hen gathers her chickens under her wings; and thou didst refuse it." [1]

Christ failed in his attempt to reach the soul of his beloved people and he came to grief again when he attempted to convince the leaders of his race.

Through the leaders one can win the streets. Have a few hundred men who are dedicated to their work, disciplined in their mind and well trained in their obedience, and you can easily sway the opinions of the multitudes and rule their destiny to your desire. The flock needs pastors or it will lose the right direction on the road. Bad shepherds are a cursed gift to a hapless nation, as we just learned from our books of history, and good ones are a blessing for the fortunes of the land.

The leader of the Jews was a well known personality, the Pharisee. A mighty figure in his time, he possessed a voice which spoke with power and authority. As a member of a religious community, he observed faithfully a rigid schedule which appointed to every hour of the day its proper use and content. Imbued with strong convictions, he followed readily a heavy set of long and arduous prayers which were attached to lengthy ceremonies, as ancient and as solemn as the Old Testament itself. Even the time for work and leisure was strictly kept according to the pages of the venerated Law. No doubt the intelligence of the Pharisee was impressive and he was well versed in his domain, the Holy Scripture. He knew by heart the chapters of the Holy Book and he explained with ease and learning what other Jews could hardly comprehend or read.

As clever politicians the Pharisees were dedicated to the glory of their nation. What helped secure the safety of the people was pursued with skill and ardor and what endangered its position was cleverly eliminated or destroyed.

[1] Matt. 23. 37.

One thing however was still missing in the notable stature of the Pharisee, something no leader can afford to miss if he aspires to greatness . . . humility. Their hearts were filled with their own glory with no place left for someone else. Their minds, trained and intelligent no doubt, became so conceited that our Lord compared them with a hidden tomb over which men walk unaware of all the danger.

As undisputed rulers of the land, the Pharisees were not in the mood to ask advice from a forlorn carpenter who did not even study in their schools. With all the multitude attuned to the wish of their supreme command, they expressed no desire to hearken to a voice which was so different from their own and far too good to be practical and true. Why should they bow if they were the ones who wore the crown? Why should they sit down at the feet of this strange master and listen humbly to the joyous tidings of this new redemption, if they alone were privileged to fathom and to announce the coming of the king of kings? Christ was, at least, a dangerous rival. The sooner they could destroy this man who called himself a God, the better for the safety of the people who did not need the message of another kingdom: "It is better that one man dies, lest the whole nation suffers."

The die was cast. With their cloth torn to pieces, the Pharisees were now beyond the stage of fear. Come what might, they would stand their ground and fight, even with the help of the despised sword of the Romans. The life and the memory of this new Redeemer was a greater hazard than the might of Caesar. Christ had to be so destroyed that no vestige of his name would be left in the mind of Israel.

Our Lord must have realized that the failure to win the leader of his beloved people was formal and complete: "You Pharisees are content to cleanse the outward part of cup and dish, while all within is running with avarice and wickedness. Fools, did not he who made the outward part make the inward too? Have nothing to do with the leaven of the Pharisees, it is all hypocrisy." [2]

Our Lord came into our midst to announce to us a kingdom which runs its borders not in this world of ours but in the bet-

[2] Luke 11. 39–40. and 12. 1.

ter realms above. For years he taught and preached about the beauty of the world to come, only to witness now that the key to this eternal kingdom was stolen by the crafty Pharisees. Not only did they shut the door of Heaven for themselves but also for the people whom he so dearly loved and whom he so gladly called his own. Thieves can be pardoned because they steal perishable goods from our markets, but how can you excuse a man who ruins a soul which is immortal? "Woe unto you, you Pharisees."

Once again our Lord was exposed to the bitter sting of painful failure. This time however the resistance did not originate in misled multitudes or in a group of wily leaders but in a single man who was still young and very rich. He was a good youth who cherished in his noble heart ideals so high that even Christ felt his attraction. Not only did the rich boy realize the obligations of his exalted position and the tremendous influence of wealth, but he was also determined with great enthusiasm to make himself a worthy subject of his calling. Ambitious enough, he dreamed of great things which he wanted to perform for himself and for the honor of his people. Christ perhaps could render him some helpful clues on how to go about it. "Master, who art so good, what good must I do to win eternal life?" Jesus looked at this honest, well groomed youth, who knelt before him, and what he saw, he liked.

"Keep the commandments!"

"Which?"

"Do not murder or commit adultery. Do not steal or bear false witness. Be not fraudulent. Honor your parents and do not forget to love thy neighbor as thyself."

"Master, all those things I have kept; what am I still missing?" Can anyone who has everything still miss something? Is fullness not necessarily combined with goodness and perfection?

"If you want to be perfect, sell what you have and give it to the poor and you will have a treasure in heaven."

This request was the climax in the swiftly developing crisis. How will the young man endure this "heavenly pressure" and how will he react to the historic call of greatness? Will his rich shoulders be strong enough to carry the weight of poverty or will his golden mind crumble under the greatest challenge of his life?

55

In order to mellow the blow our Lord did not invite the refugee from gold and silver into a dreaded "no-man's" land, where he would feel abandoned and alone, but he offered him a roof and numerous companions who were so willing and so glad to share with him the burdens and the joys of the new kingdom.

Come and follow me! This was the trump card our Lord had in his blessed hand and he laid it down before the eyes of this young man and waited. Everything depended now on the next step which the young man intended to take. All avenues of escape were blocked and the detours, which we so often seek, were tightly closed. It could only be a "yes or no." No doubt it was the turn of the young man and he took his turn. He went away sad because he had great possessions.

Christ stood there alone, defeated again by a heart which was so good and yet not good enough. Between the two there was an understanding and a love which often sparks rivalry between some kindred spirits and ends in great success and triumphs. There however the script ran differently. The love of the young man, great as it seemed, was not strong enough to bear the joy of complete abandonment. He still cherished something which was not God, and he cherished it so deeply that God had to let him go. An apostle perhaps our Lord wanted to make of him, a great apostle, daring enough to set the world on fire and to be remembered by all the coming generations. A brilliant future was offered to this youth, a future which would never turn into a past if he would be only willing to sacrifice the pleasures of the present and accept the invitation from the Lord.

Something, however, in the heart of this young man revolted against this divine overture. Something which was very subtle wounded this great adventure and turned a hopeful victory into an ominous defeat. It surely was not a sin, perhaps far from it; yet it was powerful enough to mar the chances to become a hero. At last, the love for his possessions proved stronger than the love for his own greatness. Jesus let him go. Another sheep refused its shepherd; another effort of Christ turned into failure and defeat.

It is always bitter to die with the knowledge that one has been betrayed, in the end, by one of his most trusted friends. Judas was the friend who betrayed and Christ was the man who died. To be defeated in an open battle by the sword of stronger enemies is not a shame and has to be expected, but to be delivered into the hands of the executioners through the treachery of a constant companion, this is difficult to accept and painful to endure.

Firmly determined to make a bargain with the life of his own master, Judas approached the camp of enemies and invited himself with the age old question on his greedy lips: "What will you pay me for handing him over to you? " Judas became a merchant doing business in blood and Christ became the object of the basest bargain in all history. We will never fully understand how Satan could achieve such a tremendous conquest. We may not be too wrong however if we implicate the love for money as the main source of this bitter crime.

Money is fallacious. It is saturated with temptations and with dangers. Even its handling is filled with perils. A man has to be honest and noble if he is determined to resist the lure of gold and silver. Judas obviously was not such a man. He lacked the necessary qualities needed to resist and when temptation struck his hungry passion, he had no power to refuse. What was worth the Heavens and the Earth Judas sold for a ridiculous trifle, reminding us that we are never gaining much if we betray a God.

Corrupted money never buys us peace. When Judas stared at his acquired salary of blood, he realized all of a sudden that a reward had become a curse. The silver which he had earned so desperately looked more and more like a frightful enemy who was determined to destroy its owner: "And now Judas, his betrayer, was full of remorse at seeing him condemned, so that he brought back to the chief priests and elders their thirty pieces of silver; I have sinned, he told them, in betraying the blood of an innocent man."

Friends in crimes turn enemies the moment their crime is executed. Judas lost his usefulness. He delivered his part of the bargain and the priests and elders delivered their share of the promise. No injustice was done to anyone. If Judas wanted now some sympathy and understanding, he surely had chosen the wrong place to find it: "What is that to us, they said. It concerns thee only."

The traitor was alone. Only the memory of the gruesome deed remained with him as a cruel companion into his final disaster. Although his greed had been completely routed, his love for God dared not to rise. Judas saw only an insurmountable mountain surrounded by an ever growing darkness. Can Christ forget the name of the man who sold him into the hands of his enemies? Fleeing from the temple, Judas took a rope, flung it on the branch of a tree, and hanged himself immediately. One way to finish a life which will always be remembered as the most tragic one in history.

Our Lord referring to this painful defeat in his life said the dire words: "It were better for that man if he had never been born." Only once had Christ made such a statement, and the one time he had made it, he spoke not of an enemy but of a friend who was amongst the twelve whom God had chosen to save the world.

No wonder that according to our modern physiologists, Christ's own rapid death on the cross has to be explained by a rupture of the heart, produced by mental suffering. Our Redeemer died literally of a broken heart caused by grief and failures.

Will WE ever learn?

EIGHT

Success I Like

Success is discovery. Life is filled with wonders, and these wonders are more marvelous the moment we unfold their beauty and decipher the secret of their hidden message to our mind and our ears. As the gold has to be found first and purified to be of value and of charm, so do all the mysteries of life which lie before our sight and wait for the releasing touch of their discoverer and master.

Driven forever by the desire to possess the land, man strives to gain command over his surroundings and exercise his influence and might over the destiny of his own times. Island after island, mountain after mountain fell prey to the valor of the most daring men in our midst. There is hardly left in our orbit a place which can escape the force of man's detection.

In a world where competition is so keen and ruthless, success does not arrive by invitation only. It has to be attained by magnificent efforts and secured by a dedication which knows no limitations or distractions. The prize of any victory is hard and the man of stricter discipline climbs usually the highest on the mountain of success.

Our talents and our dreams, which are so strongly guided by our birth and education, have, no doubt, a bearing and an influence on the pursuit of wealth and of prosperity; but the firm determination of the will aids most in the crusade of high ideals and brighter fortunes.

A bleak career on earth will only satisfy a weakling. The lost sheep of the flock which does not mind to stray and err will rarely discover happiness. A man who cares no more what life has in its offerings or what he can offer to life will lazily accept defeat as the inevitable fate of his existence. So accustomed to seeing the pointers of his time arrive too late, he is quite ready to give up and to surrender even before his fortress is attacked or under fire. Whatever he intends to do, he seems to do for nothing.

The man, however, who is fully conscious of his forces and determined to employ his skills to his advantage will not allow his mind to rest until he is assured that all his gifts and inspirations are hoisted to the pinnacle of glory and of fame. With great ideas of his own making he sees the face of destiny unfinished and while he is alert to his own limitations, he does not yield to broken dreams. The challenge of success is hunted until success is tamed to his own order or made to his own wish.

Success brings self-respect and honor. How changed a weary man can be if victory begins to show its gracious wings and nests amongst the heavy ruin of defeat! How bright and gay a hopeless day can end if at the threshold of the evening hours accomplishments and blessings announce their joyous entrance! The very stigma of death turns into gracious hope when shares of fortunes and of luck break the ugly curtain of a frightful night, thus changing the gloom of disappointments into rays of trust and hallowed expectations: "Listen Lord, to this cry of appeal; do not let my prayer go unheeded, though it be from the ends of the earth that I call upon thee. When my heart misgives me, thou wilt set me high up on a rock, thou wilt bring me repose; thou, my only hope, my strong tower against the assault of my enemies." [1]

To work for success is our duty, yet not to depend on it is our wisdom. If we seek glory for the sake of glory, success will hasten to abandon us as rats abandon the battered ship which is not strong enough to fight the storm. To perform well on our stage of life and not to rely upon the applause of men happens so rarely in the history of men that we write down the names of these performers and memorize their deeds and triumphs. Real greatness is equally at ease

[1] Ps. 60. 3–4.

with the harmony of victory as it is with the melody of failures. Being afraid of neither, it can quite readily endure the pressure of both.

Christ was not only a failure in his life; he was also a success. When he decided to select the men who were to carry on the mission after his departure into Heaven, he was so fortunate in the choice of his disciples that all the history of mankind is indebted to the apostles who followed Christ's appeal at once and kept their promise until their life expired.

Greatness senses greatness as timidity and smallness always find eager partners. Christ met with men who proved that they were worthy of their master. As soon as the invitation to follow was issued, it was enthusiastically accepted and immediately put to its test. Our Lord only had to call them or invite them to come and see, and they left everything behind to set out on their new road which led them into glory and to martyrdom. Their mind was clear and trustful. No detours were attached to their straight line of thinking. As soon as they heard the message from the Son of God, they were convinced that it was true. Distrust and suspicions were just as far away from all their arguments and reasons as Heaven was away from Hell. No hurdle was erected in the chambers of their hearts to deafen the song of the kingdom; nor was there created in their mind any stumbling block which could impede the grace of the Almighty: "And as he walked by the sea of Galilee, Jesus saw two brethren, Simon, who is called Peter, and his brother Andrew, casting a net into the sea (for they were fishermen); and he said to them, Come and follow me; I will make you into fishers of men. And they dropped their nets immediately and followed him." [2]

Only closeness of heart and inner understanding are able to match an order and its execution as intimately as Christ matched his command with the response of his disciples. Come follow me and at once they followed. What joy and satisfaction for the Master to see his eager pupils so ready and so well prepared to learn the greatest lesson he could ever teach to men. "Then he went further on, and saw two others that were brethren in the boat with their father Zebedee, repairing their nets, and he called them to him; whereupon they dropped the nets and left their father immediately and followed him." [3]

[2] Matt. 4. 18–20.
[3] Matt. 4. 21–22.

61

The same willingness to embrace the call for a higher mission, the same eager spontaneity to sign the promise to labor with all their daring and their power for the expansion and for the might of the kingdom of Heaven! Not one of the twelve asked for a special miracle in his honor nor was there any guarantee requested for the security and safety of their lives. They sensed the Divine the moment they saw it and they discerned the joyous tidings the instant they were preached to them. No room was left for errors or mistakes.

Such was the material Jesus needed to lay the foundation of the Church and to establish a hierarchy which initiated the celestial reign of God on earth. Such were the pillars on which the foundations of the new covenant should rest until the moment when Christ himself decited to appear again in our fiery heavens to judge the living and the dead. Jesus did not intend to let his new church rise from the stream of the past. Since the ancient institutions refused to open their gates to the spring of his glad tidings, he erected a new covenant with the apostles as the only teachers and the leaders of the morrow. Looking back now from the distance of two thousand years, we can calmly reassure the Lord that the choice he made was surely a good one.

Not all who followed Christ were as simple and as innocent as the fishermen on the lakes of Galilee. Some of the trophies Christ brought home from a dark and painful past which was so filled with shame and bitterness that none of them could cherish hopes for brighter stars on their horizons or believe in a return of happiness and peace: "Then he went out by the sea again; and all the multitude came to him, and he taught them there. And as he passed further on, he saw Levi, the son of Alphaeus, sitting at work in the customs-house, and said to him, follow me; and he rose up and followed him." [4]

Levi was a man who had his greedy pulse on the rich crossroads of the huge Roman empire. His heavy chair stood there like a hated thorn between the endless caravans and noisy merchants. If they had ever been in a position to venture their real feelings and desires, they would have burned this sign of Roman power right into the ashes of their own derision and contempt. No one likes to pay a conqueror. The Jews were no exception to this law. Yet one had to be careful and extremely cautious because the situation was fraught with secret

---

[4] Mark. 2. 13–14.

risks and open dangers. Behind the man who took their tributes and their taxes was the almighty shadow of a swift and brutal force which kept the world in order and in peace. So it was wise to endure in bitter silence what they detested with so loud a feeling of revenge.

Taxes were always high in history, and tax collectors were never famous for fighting the temptation of asking too much from the people who possessed so little. Levi did hardly anything to correct this reputation. He rested not in his demand for money until he had enough to reimburse the waiting Romans for their favors and still fill his pockets with the hard earned income of the people.

Another point, quite subtle in its nature, created difficulties for the man whom our Lord began to like. He was a traitor collaborating with the Romans who conquered Israel and ruled the Jews with terror and fear. To be neutral in a crucial fight for freedom is already bad enough, but to join the camp of enemies and still make profits by this deed of treachery is such an act of degradation that no one wished to have the slightest part in it. Levi became an outcast whom every Jew made sure to shun except this carpenter of Nazareth who found the man attractive enough to invite him to join the apostles. Not that Christ was unaware of the fact that Levi was a bleeding wound on the body of his beloved people, but he saw beneath the wound a goodness and sincerity which were far more impressive to the eyes of God than all the guilt of greed and power. So our Lord stopped, looked at him and said, "You, You come with me." Levi, hearing every word of this short and yet so triumphant sentence, left the Romans and the merchants, removed the badge of the collector and followed the new day, the day he desired so much but which he never thought would rise again on his horizon.

To prove that his decision was in earnest, he took half of the money he had accumulated and returned it quickly to the poor. One way to admit in front of the whole world that he realized that he had done wrong before and that he was determined to correct injustices and evils he had inflicted on the heart of his own people. To make the change complete, Levi became Matthew who wrote a gospel which is quite distinguished for its accuracies and for its order. No doubt, it reflects in its harmony and disposition the publican's talent to count.

There was a woman in town who was called Mary Magdalene.

About this woman, who was a public sinner, Christ said the most graceful words he could ever say about a woman in this world: "She loved so much."

No doubt Magdalene earned her praise and her distinction. The heart which was so hungry for the warm embrace of tenderness and affection desired nothing more than the gentle gift of love. Blinded, at first, by the greed of her own wily passions, Magdalene knew only the violent excitements of her flesh, which she bathed so cunningly in the scent of pleasures and corruption. But after she had met the Lord, who asked no more from her but sympathy and faith, she learned that love can be much more than lust and hunger, her beauty and her body much more than objects of desires and of sin. With inexpressible delight and ardor she totally embraced the gentle hour which brought back to her the gifts which every woman needs the most, self-respect and honor. Her friendship and her gratitude to Christ kindled the pages of the sometimes so sombre gospel with a charm and jubilation which no other woman in the records of the holy book ever reached or equaled.

Christ returned affection with affection. He loved her deeply. It was so easy for him to read her tears and understand her gay laughter because behind them was the memory of weakness and not the calculated threat of malice and of fear. The tricky arguments of the crafty Pharisees were much harder for our Lord to endure than the penitent embrace of this begging woman: "One of the Pharisees invited him to a meal; so he went into the Pharisee's house and took his place at the table. And there was then a sinful woman in the city, who, hearing that he was at table in the Pharisee's house brought a pot of ointment with her and took her place behind him at his feet, weeping; then she began washing his feet with her tears, and drying them with her hair, kissing his feet, and anointing them with the ointment. His host, the Pharisee saw it, and thought to himself, if this man were a prophet, he would know who this woman is that is touching him, and what kind of a woman, a sinner." [5]

Strange is the language of love. It speaks in peerless rhymes of enchanting poems or expresses its tender feelings in the brilliant dramas of splendor and perfection. It unfolds its intensity and ardor in the fragrance of a sea of flowers or hides its golden charm behind the

[5] Luke 7. 36–39.

64

wings of silence and seclusion. Love can erupt into storms of dangers and destruction, or it can burst into the passionate flame of a kiss in which the whole world is embraced and yet so totally excluded. When Mary Magdalene, at last, found the Master whom she could love and serve forever, her heart began to weep and tears rolled from her grateful eyes down the feet of our Lord. Weeping freed her heart from all the heavy burdens, and her tears appeased the sorrow which she still sensed about the shadows of her past. Now she found the answer to the greatest question of her life. How to love? She found Christ.

Next to Christ there was a good thief hanging on the cross, waiting, as our Saviour, for the releasing hand of death. Not well matched in the beginning of the drama on the hill of Calvary, he slowly closed the gap which separated him from his eternal friend and heavenly Redeemer. The excruciating pains of flesh revived in him the biting memories of crimes which he had committed in the past and which he never did regret. He knew so clearly now there was not much to brag about the deeds of years gone by, since they were bad and rotten from the beginning to the very end. Yet, as any other criminal, he toiled perhaps with the idea that they would never catch him in his flight from justice. Why not go on in his profession until the last day of his life? But luck, his famous luck, ran out on him at last. They caught him and the punishment was obvious, death by crucifixion. One way to erase a menace which refused to be cured.

Death, in its coming, clears the path of ambiguities and falsehoods. Who can afford the luxury of cheating death? Who can risk the danger of meeting death behind the cover of a mask? The good thief realized perhaps for the first time in his life that the exact account of his achievements was a bleak and wretched number. Wherever he gazed with his dying glance, he saw the ruins of his pitiful career staring back into his face. He knew that these ruins were his; at this greatest moment in his life, he was willing to admit it. He sensed that the cross on which he hanged was deserved. Rebuking another thief who cursed his fate ,he said: "Hast thou no fear of God, when thou art undergoing the same sentence? And we justly enough; we receive no more than the due reward for our deeds; but this man has done nothing amiss." [6] Something different began to stir up in his broken life, something so new and yet so old, a sense of justice. I pay my

[6] Luke 23. 41–42.

debts to God and I pay my debts to those whose life I made so miserable. I pay for my crimes to find my peace at last. A sense of justice graces any man, especially a bad one.

The hardest step in life is taken when one begins to break one's pride. The good thief opened up his wounds and let them bleed so that by bleeding they could heal. His first confession relieved his soul from the iron grip which his guilt had held on him for so many years. He felt free again as any child of God who gained forgiveness of his sins. Now, with his new found courage he dared to make another step, cautious in the beginning but glorious in the end. Not used to asking for anything, he just begged for a remembrance from this innocent stranger whom he admired more and more: "Lord, remember me when thou comest into thy kingdom." This was all he asked, a remembrance. Sensing the opportunity to change defeat into triumph, Our Lord turned his head towards the begging thief and said: "I promise thee, this day thou shalt be with me in Paradise." [7]

God made his decision. His first companion for this triumphant entrance into Heaven was selected. It was not one of those honest pagans who waited so long to perceive the light which is eternal. Nor was it one of those serious prophets who yearned for centuries to realize the fulfillment of his hidden dream. Nor was it blessed Joseph who cared so well for all the needs of Christ and Mary. It was this despised and hated criminal who merely lost everything but found his sense of justice. The greatest treasure on earth, Heaven, was promised to him so that he did not have to steal it.

It was about the sixth hour, and darkness lay over the whole land. The earth was deeply shaken to its depths. Terror and fear gripped the hearts of the horrified Jews while the gambling Romans began to ponder over the happenings which were so strange and unexpected. Many hurried away from the bloody hill of Calvary, haunted by the biting pangs of a guilty conscience.

The good thief was resigned and serene. A deep peace came over his pain-racked body and absolved from all his crimes by the High priest of the new covenant, he was ready to die in triumph on the sign of shame.

Nothing more of him is known. His name Dismas is preserved in manuscript and in tradition. Behind his name, however, stands one

[7] Luke 23. 43.

of the most beautiful triumphs which our Lord achieved in his career, a success which was worth the noble efforts of a God.

The tax collector, the harlot and the thief are three strong personalities which will always be remembered in the pages of the holy book. Their faces were borne of intense suffering and bitterness while their soul arose from the darkness of great sins. As different as their cradle may have been, they all agree in the enthusiasm with which they echoed forth the call of their Redeemer. Unlike Judas, their lips did not betray their Master. They never forgot that Christ had given their new life eternal happiness and glory.

While writing about successes in the life of Christ, we could never finish such a chapter without mentioning two other trophies which our Lord brought home for his collection, YOU and me.

NINE

Suffering I Dislike

The dream of man is forever different from the dream of God. While we are always inclined to adorn our expectant future with a long and golden string of joy and gayish laughter, our Lord cherishes ideas of different colors. The moment we decorate our hearts with glittering toys and delightful pleasures our Redeemer hammers diligently on a cross, making it ready for shoulders which are, without doubt, so much our own. If we were ever free to compose our own story of life, we would certainly oblige our secret desires and erase gently but inexorably the days of pain and suffering. Ardently we would fashion a fascinating tale of glorious triumphs with us as glamorous heroes who conquered with our glittering swords the threats of blood and persecution. So our script would run for every hour of the day, and not one minute would be free for lamentations and for beastly cries.

The greatest Leader of the universe possessed only one weapon which He bequeathed to HIS soldiers — the Cross. When He commanded His faithful apostles to step into the four corners of the universe, to preach the joyous tidings to the ears of every face and to baptize the skin of every color, He gave them nothing else for their long and dangerous journey but the memory of a shameful death

68

on a despised and bloody cross. "Father, why hast Thou forsaken me?" This heaven-piercing shout was the strange melody which strengthened the weary minds of the disciples and tightened their courage in death and persecution. When two of His disciples lost the fire of their faith and decided to return home, Our Lord joined their weary steps and argued with their gloomy minds, saying to them reproachfully: "Too slow of wit, too dull of heart to believe all those sayings of the prophets! Was it not to be expected that the Christ should undergo these sufferings and so enter into His glory?" Was it not the strategy of the "divine command" to lead Christ over the nails of the cross into the bliss of heavenly felicity? Even if it is true that human ingenuity can never fathom the reasons why suffering and pain have to exist, it is equally true that we possess the most beautiful reasons to accept it. If it was good enough for God, it is good enough for me. "I am the wheat of Christ," prayed one of our great saints; "may I be ground by the teeth of beasts, that I may be found pure bread."

There are only two hills which top the surface of the ground we walk on — Tabor and Calvary. One was chosen by God for His resplendent transfiguration, while the other became the place of His death. Both hills rise before our searching eyes, majestic and imposing, and beg to be the choice of our hearts. Both cross the path of our life and force the mind to a decision. Which of these two will be our first choice? Is it not true that our *favorite* is forever Tabor, the mountain of joy, which rises like a mighty dome into the blue of the sky and rules the peaceful silence of the surrounding hills? "And he was transfigured in their presence, his face shining like the sun, and his garments becoming white as snow. And all at once they had sight of Moses and Elias conversing with him. Then Peter said aloud to Jesus, "Lord, it is well that we should be here; if it pleases thee, let us make three arbors in this place, one for thee, one for Moses and one for Elias." [1]

It is so deep a desire, perhaps almost an instinct of man, to seek and embrace God in His glory, adore Him and worship the Lord as long as He reflects the stunning beauty of the sun and mirrors the brilliant white of the gentle snow. On such triumphant grounds we love to dwell, to build our roofs and to plant our cities, with a pow-

[1] Matt. 17. 2–4.

erful God as our mighty King and undisputed Ruler. On Tabor the apostles liked to remain; from Calvary they rushed away. Splendor was balm to their hungry hearts, the doom of death frightened their trembling lips into silence and defeat. When Jesus bowed His head and yielded up His spirit, there was only one man under the cross — John, the apostle whom our Lord loved so much. He was courageous enough to witness the deadly struggle of the Divine Victim as he was strong enough to accept Mary as his mother. Other apostles trembled behind locked doors in fear of being hunted down by the victorious sword of their prevailing enemies. Judas went away, put a rope around his neck, and hanged himself on the branch of a tree. "I have betrayed innocent blood," was the ugly sentence of death which Judas himself wrote in his bitter despair. This tragic sentence remains in our midst as a warning to those who are ready again to peddle God for a greater share of their ugly profits. No other name in history reveals to us how low a man can bend to reach money, as no other name is so cursed as the name of Judas. That name will never be forgotten. ·

The sufferings we have to endure will pass, but the way we suffered will forever leave an imprint in the soul of man, which no one can erase. If we accept our share of the cross with stoic minds and hardened lips, ready to bow under the cleansing whip of God the Almighty as we bow under the heat of the day, then we can not expect to feel the aiding grace from Heaven above, nor will the strength of our faith alleviate the weight of our painful burden. Endurance is not like sanctification. No one demands us to love what is bitter, but to accept with holy resignation the tearful gift of God. This is the sign of faith. "The sun was darkened, and the veil of the temple was torn in the midst;" and Jesus said, crying with a loud voice, "Father, into thy hands I commend my spirit."

As the burned-out soil needs the gentle touch of long-awaited rain to blossom forth into the most gorgeous harvest, so our arid souls need our blessed tears to be cleansed, deepened and strengthened. Men who have never suffered might easily remain immature and childish even to the embarrassing degree in which they cease to be men. There are profound depths in our hearts which are dormant and are not yet awakened. The power of suffering has to penetrate there to break the hardened rind wide open and bring those precious depths into existence. Not that we deny that suffering can destroy human character and wreck the harmony of mind, yet many of us never reach the fullness and maturity of character and personality without the help of pain and trial. We do not imply that each and everyone has to endure hardships and tribulations to enter the kingdom of eternal bliss and happiness; but if God in His all-embracing love and wisdom has decreed that our soul is to be saved under the shadow of the cross, then this cross will come, pierce us and remain with us until its heavenly mission is fully achieved. Only the tragic rebellion of the human mind which ends so often in suicide, or the pitiful collapse of human courage which is despair, can prevent suffering from making our life, deep, rich and beautiful.

The moment we are called upon to meet the cross, that very moment we are most alone. Friends and enemies retire from the horizon of our life and watch us from the sidelines with pretty flowers in their restless hands. Our own face, heroic or detestable as it may be, will steadily surge to the surface and predominate the scene. The worth of our name, our inner strength or feebleness, our character, personality, or faith, all that we really are or pretend to be, will almost suddenly break through its hiding place and face "the open." Never before was the delicate question "Who am I?" so candidly put on the market as in this crucial moment. Perhaps never before was this important question so decisively answered than in the painful hours when our cunning instincts and our sensual drives were firmly tamed and solidly curbed by the greater power of a loving Master and by the stern requests of a demanding Lord. When we are tested by suffering, we cannot lie even if we should try. We have to write our name as God spells it and not as we fancy it in our wishful dreams. Perhaps our heart will faint and tremble like the heart of a coward, or our hands will shake like the inner world of a weakling who never said "No" to his rapacious hunger; or we might surprise everyone with a calm and tranquility which have secretly grown and blossomed in our patience and in our self-denials. Some disappoint us in the tragic call of Calvary while others rise to a greatness which we never suspected to be in their hearts. A few even approach their hour of death with an inner harmony and peace which no power on earth is able to reach and no sword is strong enough to split apart. Deeply convinced that the physical damage has no power to penetrate beneath their skin, they suffer in their sensible flesh but keep their disciplined mind in tranquility and hope. Firmly founded in their precious faith, they remain unhurt and perhaps become more perfect in their soul the more the outer frame is wrecked. Writing to the Corinthians who were in distress, St. Paul begs them: "No, we do not play the coward; though the outward part of our nature is being worn down, our inner life is refreshed from day to day. This light and momentary affliction brings with it a reward multiplied in every way, loading us with everlasting glory; if only we will fix our eyes on what is unseen, not on what we can see. What we can see lasts for the moment; what is unseen is eternal.[2]

The cross of Calvary is not blessed because it is a cross; it is holy because Christ carried it on His wounded shoulders. In our religion suffering is never sought for the sake of suffering but only as a means — a bitter means — to secure a better end. Even the perfect ones in our annals — call them saints — might deeply dislike their open wounds and wish they never had them; yet they accept them reverently and in submission, and even bring them closer to their lips to kiss them because behind the open wounds, they discern the mysterious love of God which they never fail to acknowledge and to adore. Our Lord, Who never laughed at us, was able to weep over our cities, cry over our tombs and share the sorrow of the widow who loses her only child. On Mount Olivet He Himself was surrounded by a sadness so piercing and profound that it reached the very abyss of annihilation and approached the very hall of death. Blood trickled down His frightened face and His countenance was changed beyond recognition. He confided to his sleepy apostles that His soul was ready to die with sorrow, and He begged them to stay awake and to pray with Him. What a brutal nightmare Our Lord sustained on this fateful mountain only to be prepared for a journey into deeper darkness which found its deadly burst on Calvary. Here the scorn of the rabble extinguished totally the flame of eternal love and pierced a heart which always wanted to love, but never knew how to hate. "Let us hold fast then," writes St. Paul, "by the faith we profess. We can claim a great high priest, and one who has passed right up through the heavens, Jesus, the Son of God. It is not as if our high priest was incapable of feeling for us in our humilia-

[2] II Cor. 4. 16–18.

72

tions; he has been through every trial, fashioned as we are, only sin-less. Let us come boldly, then, before the throne of grace, to meet with mercy, and win that grace which will help us in our needs." [3]

With Christ on our side the worst of our pain is conquered and the sting of our open wounds is taken out. The knowledge that God, Who has suffered Himself, is our companion and our protector, and that nothing can hurt us against His will — this blessed knowledge will not fail to strengthen the nerves and cool the fever and appease the storm which threaten our life with danger and destruction. No matter what our trials and sufferings for the moment appear to be, our life as a whole is in the hands of God Whom we trust more than any other power in this universe. The greedy hands of cold despair will never reach the blessed land of our sorrows.

Humble patience can absorb the greatest measure of a man who has learned the lessons of his limitations and is prepared to pay the price for them without becoming disillusioned or sarcastic; such a man will benefit the most from the raw and sombre climate of the heights of Calvary. He will not easily be tempted to impose his wounds on others, nor will he climb the stage of life and proclaim himself a martyr. If sympathy is gently offered to his agonizing hours, he accepts it gratefully without yearning for too much of this sweetest medicine. Convinced that he alone is tested in the stormy battle, he lets the others go away. "So, once more, Jesus asked them, 'Who is it you are looking for?' And when they said, 'Jesus of Nazareth,' he answered, 'I have told you already that I am Jesus. If I am the man you are looking for, let these others go free.' " [4]

It is far more strenuous for human endurance to accept the drawn out monotony of slight and secret suffering than the short and violent threat of a terrifying disaster. One may easily be a magnificent hero in the thick of a glorious battle only to become a helpless child with a painful tooth. Such a reverse is not at all surprising since it is always easier for men to be outstanding in the hour of a tremendous challenge than to be great and heroic in little trials and temptations. In the end, which is so inevitable, all of us must accept the bitter fact that we become a burden to the people whom we love so

[3] Heb. 4. 14–16.
[4] John 18. 7–8.

73

dearly. When the aging years commence to write their ugly wrinkles, when strength and vigor fail to rise, when our heart, fatigued and restless, begins to murmur and to sigh, then we have to learn to accept from other hands relief and comfort. To be dependent on the aid of others might well be the hardest lesson which some in our midst must learn before they die. The full acceptance of our helplessness and even uselessness can bring to us the holy grace we need so much to make us worthy in the sight of our merciful Father in heaven.

Whoever has passed through a storm bravely and successfully is better able to discover and perceive the sufferings of others. Sorrow breaks the deafness of our hearts wide open. A soul which has endured the bitter darkness is cleansed enough to grasp the tears of others. Compassion is the most beautiful harvest which we can gather from the blooming fields of our sorrows. Only the beast in us, as the beast in the steaming jungles, trots away from the heart-rending yells of agony and flees so quickly from the stench of open wounds. Some grow so cold and snobbish at the sight of pains and trials that they themselves begin to doubt whether or not their heart is still alive and beating. It needs much greater love and deeper courage to touch the wounds and heal them than to shun forever the glorious view of the cross. Have not a few of us allowed our very soul to wither away and to die before the hour of death? With the greatest treasure of life lost, we keep nothing else in our greedy fingers but our hoarded money. Like the Romans of old we want to gamble the shadow of the cross, deeply set in our wily heart to win at any price the bigger share of the booty. "They divide my spoils among them, cast lots for my garments." [5]

On Holy Saturday, the vigil of Easter, the impressive ceremonies of our holy faith have a dramatic beginning. The church, clothed in darkness and silence, suddenly begins to vibrate with life again through the solemn entrance of the priest who is accompanied by his loyal altar boys and surrounded by the assembly of his faithful flock. A hush of expectancy, like the silence before great events, is spread over this holy drama. Then, with a voice which is about to assume something of the joy and excitement of the impending triumph of our Lord and Saviour, the priest begins to sing. "Lumen

[5] Matt. 27. 35.

Christi," (Light of Christ); and the voices of the faithful swiftly answer, equally forceful, "Deo gratias," (Thanks be to God). The priest steps forward towards the middle of the holy hall, carrying cautiously a huge candle, and intones again with a voice slightly higher than before, "Lumen Christi"; and again the faithful are ready to reply to his challenging call, "Deo gratias." For a third and last time the celebrant moves ahead closer to the sanctuary which is still veiled in dark obscurity, and again sings with the highest and most joyous voice the reassuring melody, "Lumen Christi"; and like a powerful echo the answer surges through the multitude, "Deo gratias." With the echo of this last call still ringing in the air, a triumphant burst of light breaks the shroud of darkness, disperses the heavy gloom of Good Friday, and the blessed sanctuary is ready and set to echo forth the brilliant message of the triumphant Resurrection.

This remarkable scene is repeated so often in the menacing storms of our own existence. At first darkness surrounds us, heavy thick darkness, with no ray of hope bursting through the threatening clouds. Blinded by our sorrow we do not perceive the light, and numbed by our pain we do not reach the rays of trust and confidence. All we hear are the screams of agony, the mad yells of despair, and the waning cries of death. "Lumen Christi — Light of Christ," the only light which has the power to break through every chain of despair, brightens up the edge of darkness, and sheds on our bleeding wounds a peace which no one on earth can destroy. "Deo gratias — Thanks be to God," for our faith. Thanks be to God we can believe that on the other side of bitterness, our sufferings are crowned by the mysterious love of a merciful Father in heaven. With this strong and blessed belief in our heart we can welcome suffering as a desirable guest in the room of our life. But without this holy faith, darkness grows only darker and darker.

TEN

Where Confidence And Courage Meet

If some refuse to trust in God's omnipotence because they are not able to believe in his existence, they only draw a logical conclusion which we do not exactly applaud but which we can readily understand. If some accept however the reality of God and still are frightened by the powers of this world, they are either foolish in their hearts or strangely ignorant of God's decisive power and of the mighty span of his tremendous wisdom.

True confidence has its roots in strong convictions which are born of deep faith and trust in God alone. Fear however begins to flourish in our life when real belief has lapsed into oblivion and human calculations take over the complete command. The man who willingly bids God farewell and seeks no solace from the grace of Heaven is but a frail and easy prey to all the cunning of the moment. Deep trust in God, however, creates the favorable climate in which the storms of life lose all their threats of evil and turn into a challenge which we are strong enough to conquer. If once a German general could say to his embattled soldiers, "Stay close at my side, nothing ever happens to me"; how much more a Christian who follows a God who conquered all his enemies: "What gives them confidence? Weapons of war and their own daring. Ours to trust in his omnipotence, who with a single nod both these our adversaries and the world besides can undo." [1]

We modern people, as we so joyously call our generation, find ourselves often bewildered and perturbed by the tensions of the race we are set to win. Pricked by strange fears and wounded by deep anxieties, we lose the inherent sense of tranquility and peace which supported us so well in critical moments of the past. Not that the years of yesterday were full of bliss and joys, we never claimed such glorious perfection for the past, but whatever they brought to our doors of life we were in a position to accept and strong enough to endure without the sense of doom or imminent disaster.

The situation of today is quite different. Our world is wounded and fatigued. So many amongst us are ready to surrender to a fate which is unknown to us in its ultimate demands and in its final errors. We might have pawned our final security to a total atomic holocaust which has but few survivors, or we might have entrusted our peace and our salvation to the brightest future mankind ever knew.

The stunning achievements of human ingenuity and skill have doubtless lightened the boring weight of our daily burdens but they have also complicated our mode of living to a degree that man is not exactly master anymore in the home of his own creation. Man is afraid of his own inventions because they grow and grow in their dimension and their power while he seems to diminish, day by day, in stature, influence and power. Conditions were revolutionized for the better and we acknowledge that with gratitude, but in the process of success and triumphs man degenerated to a moral level which is as low and vulgar as hardly any other on the scales of history. If we would ask ourselves why we are not more cheerful and at ease with all the opulence at our reach, we would find it hard to put in words the difficulties we experience. But we do know that life is for almost all of us a source of tensions and of strain to which we have to adjust ourselves although we are quite often ill-prepared for this enormous task.

No doubt our ancestors experienced uncomfortable moments too. We know that well enough and all of us are rather proud about the

[1] 2 Mach. 8. 18.

way they met their challenge and forced all dangers into flight. Not only did they have to cope with strange surroundings and defy the threats of enemies and beasts, but they had also to endure extremes of climate and of hunger before the land was safe and conquered. Surely their share of perils and of risks was great, but they still could hide before the onslaught of the brewing storm and flee to safety when disaster struck the village or destroyed the roaming herds. Their harried soul had never lost the ray of hope, which our modern counterpart has lost completely. No roof is left to hide in the atomic age. The bomb, whose breath is hydrogen, is violent enough to tear apart with lethal fury the steel of every fortress and split to shreds the concrete walls of safety and protection. What power all the newer "super-weapons" will possess no one can clearly fathom yet. They look quite innocent on our drawing boards, but put once into action they will be violent enough to annihilate our planet and make of our shelters lovely tombs.

To say that weapons of such terror will never be released on men is just a little more than men dare to believe. From the experience of our past we all have learned another lesson which hardly anyone of us likes to forget. There really was not yet an enemy who had the weapons to destroy but did not use them. That our warriors are different must first be put to test before we can believe it. Too much is now at stake to trust in words or ink alone.

What kind of hope is left for us in this absorbing threat of total annihilation? What kind of alternative, if any, remains on our side?

The possibility of absolute extinction offers to man total despair in humanity or complete confidence in divinity. No other choice is left to our begging hands. Whether we realize it or not, our decision has narrowed to an "eternal yes" or to an "eternal no." Perfect faith or total unbelief are the day and night which offer our soul a harbor. Atheism which stands for the "eternal NO" is a message without hope because it is a denial without love. True love has vanished from the paradise of communism and what is left from all their promises can never blaze the fire of redemption. Materialism, veiled or open, brutal or smooth, is for the dream of man a hopeless disappointment. The most we can expect from its seductive glitter is ashes, ashes and more dust. Strong faith in God, however, stimulates courage which moves not only hills and mountains but also makes the darkest hours bearable and holy.

The truth of God's solicitude and care is one of the most beautiful and consoling revelations in our age of tension and of threat. To know and to be convinced that nothing, really NOTHING happens to us which is not willed or permitted by God for the greater good of our imperishable soul, this precious knowledge and this deep conviction can yield to our mind and body such courage and composure that even in this age of super-bombs we can remain serene and fearless. Although we are left alert and sensitive to threats of dangers and of death as any animal which senses perils of its own destruction, the worst of it is conquered and the sting of it removed by the thought that God is our loving keeper and that nothing can hurt us without his will. How can it fail to steady the excited nerves, cool the fever and appease the fret if we are deeply conscious that no matter how great the danger for the moment appears to be, our life, as a whole, is in the hands of a supreme power in which we can totally confide: "Courage and a man's part, that is what I ask of thee; no room for fear and shrinking back, when the Lord, thy God is at thy side wherever thou goest." [2]

May we remember however that the victory of God is not always interpreted in equal fashion as our victories on earth; quite often the only thing they have in common would be the spelling of the word. In the book of history a triumph means a gain at the expense of our enemies or a defeat we inflicted upon our opponents, who failed to measure up to the ingenuities of our resources or counted badly the amount of talents we possessed. The very moment the assailant takes to flight is called success in our view of life and if we hear sweet melodies of praise for our daring feat, we take such nice acclaims for granted.

The victory of Christ arose from a world of different proportions. For him success meant failure and victory had the design of clear defeat. A shameful death made him a conqueror and crucified between two thieves he died as king of our universe. Since Calvary has found its place on our maps, the sword alone can not decide the spoils. We learned that there is more to triumphs and failures than our eyes

[2] Jos. 1. 9.

can see and our mind can measure. There is much more to death than the fatal message of defeat and ignominy. To those who understand, explanations are not necessary, but to those who have no belief, explanations are of no help.

The Christian is convinced that again and again he is sent out on a journey which he is never able to complete since all his steps remain forever a beginning. He is aware of duties and responsibilities which are his own, his own alone, and yet ALONE he is not strong enough to master them. Better than any other man the faithful one realizes that all his steps are fraught with dangers and though he is willing to accept the challenge, he never will enjoy the thrill of ultimate success. To sell one's soul for final triumphs here on earth is surely as foolish as to sell one's faith for titles or for better money. To live for victory alone and flee the message of defeat is purely a dream which they embrace most stubbornly who never understood the message of the cross: "Too slow of wit, too dull of heart, to believe all those sayings of the prophets! Was it not to be expected that the Christ should undergo these sufferings, and enter so into his glory?" [3]

Once confidence in God has found its entrance into our heart, it will produce its consequences and show its proper offspring; yet it will never erase the sense of fear in our life. It is perhaps correct to say that once a man rejects the gift of love he seldom finds it back again; but to apply this statement to a coward and claim that after one rejection he will never find again his courage is totally unjust and dangerous. Who did not become a coward once? Who did not flee from challenges which wanted to be conquered? Who was always a hero?

It is only natural to be afraid in certain situations. Our fright may range from personal afflictions into the vast and mysterious realm of the unknown. The man who tells us that he never entertained the feelings of timidity and dread might be the very man who lacks imagination or hides behind the cover of a lie. To expect that trust in God will bring immunity to our feelings is such an unheard-of luxury that even God himself could not afford to buy it: "And now he grew dismayed and distressed: My soul, he said to them, is ready to die with sorrow; do you abide here, and keep watch." [4] If Christ whose heart was full of trust in God went through

[3] Luke 24. 25–26. [4] Mark 14. 34.

80

this long and agonizing journey, how much more we whose confidence in God is often frail and foolish. The inner force of our soul, which alone sustains the outer manifestations, can often go from highest exultations into the depth of misery and anguish. A few might even come close to the point where they are tempted to shout into the dark and angry sky "O God, O God, why hast thou forsaken me?"

One guest however is never allowed to cross the threshold of the faithful — despair. Our reliance on the love of the heavenly father who never abandons his beloved child, will not permit us to walk this hopeless road where madness lies and where the travelers are left alone and stranded. Despair is the deadly fruit Christians never have to eat. It is reserved for those who lost the one thing man can not afford to lose — faith: "Reckless of unshod feet, of parching throat, thou criest out despairingly, Return I cannot; to alien gods all my heart is vowed, and I must follow still!" [5] It was only Judas who thought that there was no salvation anymore for him and hanged himself on a tree. Only about this man of despair did our Lord say what was so hard to hear: "It would have been better he were not born."

As a wrong concept of life produces a strange and warped thought of death, so does a wrong idea of faith create a faulty notion of true confidence and courage. If our opponents show quite often greater stamina in defying God than we show in defending him, it proves that their convictions are more deeply rooted than our belief in God's eternal revelation. Although we are not responsible that divine ideals must triumph all over our universe, we still have the sacred duty to struggle for their conquest with all the might of our soul. To perform miraculous and stunning deeds is often far beyond our strength and calling, but to practice fearlessly what we believe is true, this is the holy obligation from which no one can excuse himself. If we would only wait for the arrival of the moment when our name is flashed with glamor and with heroism on to the screen of history, we might be waiting all our life and just do nothing. But if we project our solid convictions into the stern demands of our daily life, we may create an atmosphere where God can rule and triumph without the glitter and

[5] Jer. 2. 25.

the noise of boisterous exhibitions. Perhaps such hidden courage and unsung fidelity demand far greater confidence in God than crusaders need, who swing their swords in open warfare: "God has chosen what the world holds foolish, so as to abash the wise, God has chosen what the world holds weak, so as to abash the strong. God has chosen what the world holds base and contemptible, nay, has chosen what is nothing, so as to bring to nothing what is now in being." [6]

If it is true to say that our cowardice and our failures can not destroy the eternal values of the Gospel, it is equally correct to state that our errors and our deficiencies accumulate so much dust and dirt that the eternal gold of our message can not be recognized anymore by those who seek its excellency and search for its abundant worth. Can we blame a man who sincerely looks for God but can not find him because he has found us? The practical materialism, so prevalent amongst us Christians, puts our so-called confidence in God "to laughter and to shame." Perhaps WE are the very reason why God is so little loved today in so many parts of our world? What we have lost so carelessly of the great heritage which once was ours, the modern enemies have zealously recovered and THEY present it now to a hungry world as the pearls of their wisdom. Do not the wily slogans of our enemies reflect a perfect image of the passions we ourselves projected into their envy and into their greed? Where are the Christians today who are willing to endure a brutal death under the claws of hungry lions before they would betray to tyrants their convictions and ideals? Could St. Paul write about us what he wrote about the invincible faith and courage of God's beloved children? "Theirs was the faith which subdued kingdoms, which served the cause of right, which made promises come true. They shut the mouths of lions, they quenched raging fire, swords were drawn on them, and they escaped. How strong they became, who till then were weak, what courage they shewed in battle, how they routed invading armies. One and all gave proof of their faith; yet they never saw the promise fulfilled; for us, God had something better in store. We were needed to make the history of their lives complete." [7]

[6] 1 Cor. 1. 27–28.
[7] Heb. 11. 33–35 and 39–40.

The spiritual vacuum which we so cowardly created and which lies all over our Christian lands has become a fertile breeding ground for the promises and manifestoes of our revolutionaries and dictators. One has to be potentially good and loyal even to realize that it is not enough to drift along with the attractions of bigger movies and of better food. One has to love ideals before one is willing to die for one. Many a communist would make perhaps an excellent Christian if he would only find one he could imitate. Thousands more would never join the ranks of hatred and brutality if they would only see, with their own eyes, unselfish deeds and sacrifices born of indomitable faith and confidence in God's omnipotence and love. If communism spreads much more in our day than in any other period of history, it is not only on account of bad economic conditions, we had such conditions before, but on account of the presence of millions of Christians who betrayed their sacred heritage and sold again their faith for thirty pieces of good silver.

St. Francis of Assisi and the Russian Vladimir Lenin were perhaps not so far apart at the outset of their journey as Franciscans and Communists seem to be in our days. Both of these two different men grew up in a secure and comfortable milieu able to look forward to a cozy and untroubled future which would have provided a rich and carefree time to come. Yet they failed to fulfill the hopes of their surroundings since their own dreams were different from the desires of all others. What was regarded as attractive and desired, both detested as deficient and repulsive. When others spoke of preservation of their social standards, these two began to think of changes and reforms. Soon, they revolted. Francis and Lenin refused to wear the golden chains which might have been a necklace for a few but fetters of despair for many. A war was silently declared against their own society, a war in which they differed in their strategy. One carried the idea of violence and courage against HIMSELF and he became the greatest saint. The other believed in a social upheaval by violence against OTHERS and he became a bloody tyrant.

A coward is not exactly a pretty sight. Neither God nor man is thrilled by his alarming presence. Uncertain of himself, a timid man becomes unpredictable in his actions and unreliable in his

83

speech. Offered a choice between the two, he prefers forever the safety of a speech to the challenge of an action. Tolerable in times of peace when the harm and damage he inflicts are slight, he turns into a danger in periods of war when his timidity and indecision stir up disasters around the men in the same trench. He even might begin to start a rout and lose a battle which otherwise could surely have been won. If he, at last, decides to use the sword, he will cut only his own flesh and ready to apply the wrath of his indignation, he burns the roof of his own dwelling.

A nation suffers intensely and even risks to perish if a coward is allowed to rise to power and to rule the fate of the land. With his timid breath, the life of the country will diminish and wither slowly into the gray of gloom. Sensing his obvious weakness, such a ruler will forever suspect demands of courage and of strength and foster what is frail and timid. Not powerful enough to conquer yet vain enough to refuse defeat, he is perturbed by one as much as by the other. If, at last, his folly is exposed, he rather lays to waste the nation before he would surrender to a better man. What such a land has to endure in sufferings is not the greatest of calamities, but what such a nation has to miss is tragic: "Bad conscience takes to its heels, with none in pursuit; fearless as a lion the unreproved heart." [8]

True courage is like a solid nail; the harder you hit it the deeper it goes. Times of suffering and persecution were always for our sacred faith times of growth and progress, whereas long and prosperous peace lay heavy on the pillars of the Church. Built as man is, he thrives on challenges. The Christian is surely no exception to this attractive rule. Take the challenge away from a man and you take away his heart. Give to Christianity benevolent surroundings for too long a time and you give her an enemy which she is unable to subdue. Faith does not like to be a thing we take for granted. The moment we fail to honor and defend our holy belief it seems to disappear and leave us abandoned and alone. Yet, as we all know so well, faith has never reached more stunning heights than when it bled under the edge of persecution: "Do not be surprised, beloved, that this fiery ordeal should have

[8] Prov. 28. 1.

befallen you, to test your quality; there is nothing strange in what is happening to you. Rather rejoice, when you share in some measure the sufferings of Christ; so joy will be yours and triumph, when his glory is revealed." [9]

Not only the Caesars of old learned the glorious chapters which Christian confidence and courage wrote into the annals of their history. Our modern tyrants, too, studied carefully the intimate connections which exist between brutal persecutions and the glorious triumph of religion. Convinced, at last, that vulgar force alone avails so little, they returned their savage sword into the scabbard and concentrated on the human mind where faith is rooted like a fortress on a rock. To break this mind of man — not to destroy it — this is the modern battle cry of our thirsty enemies. If they have met with some success in their most ruthless robbery, it was not due to their victims' lack of confidence in God, but due to drugs and glaring light which turned the character of man into a stammering puppet. Tamed lips finally may readily confess what those brutal masters like so much to hear: that God is dead and that the Gospel of the future is written by the self-styled prophets of atheistic communism.

For the moment, the influence and power of our faithless enemies is formidable and well organized. Still winning in the never resting contest for the supremacy of the human mind, they pride themselves that they have emptied the skies, emptied our sanctuaries, emptied the human soul and finally emptied themselves. They broadcast that more conflicts are to be expected, that more battles have to be won before they can declare that God is totally defeated. In their own mind, however, they have no doubt that the hour of their triumph is in the cards of history.

How little do they realize that they are fighting a battle which they lost almost the moment it began. It is not a contest between a stronger and a weaker enemy; nor is it a match between swords and sharper swords. In the final analysis, it is an encounter between the almighty God and his helpless creature. Can man ever find a chance to conquer God, or tell him that he does not exist? Can he ever hope to destroy a heart which only wanted

[9] 1 Peter 4. 12–13.

to love and to be loved? "There is no God above us, is the fond thought of reckless hearts. Warped natures everywhere and hateful lives, there is not an innocent man amongst them." [10]

Chesterton said once that even a watered-down Christianity is hot enough to boil all modern society to rags. We enjoy this daring statement and we applaud it; yet we would like to add another element to its impressive meaning. If a watered-down edition of our sacred faith contains enough intensity and ardor to conquer the threats of our modern enemies, how much more an ideal Christianity which we desire and for which we pray. Is there an enemy in this world who is strong enough to hurt a man who trusts God more than any other power of this earth? Is there a force in this world which is mighty enough to destroy the peace and the inner freedom of a saint: "God is here to deliver me; I will go forward confidently, and not be afraid; source of my strength, theme of my praise, the Lord has made himself my protector. So, rejoicing, you shall drink deep from the fountain of deliverance; singing, when that day comes, Praise the Lord, and call upon his name, tell the story of his doings among all the nations, keep the majesty of his name in grateful remembrance." [11]

Faith is not a wide and powerful stream which will carry us by sheer necessity to a never ending bliss in Heaven. What we make of this glorious heritage will, in the final analysis, give our heart its courage and its devotion.

Let me keep my promise to you O Lord, so that I can vindicate your trust in me. May the last thing which will die in me be my confidence in God.

[10] Ps. 52. 2.
[11] Is. 12. 2–4.

ELEVEN

Peace Be Still

No man is so calm and quiet as the man who died. Peacefully he lies there, in a tranquility and stillness which is so impressive and unique that we look in vain for any duplicate in our lively midst. No sound of word is allowed to skip over the threshold of his frigid lips nor are his lifeless eyes permitted to signal any message, except the one, of course, we never wish to learn, of life's fragility and emptiness. Even the gloomy morgue, where death is for the last time decorated like a hero, is a secluded world of quietness in which we hardly dare to breath, afraid we might disturb the solemn atmosphere which shrouds the heavy walls up to their very ceilings. Silence must be at its best in these surroundings, we might begin to think; and our judgment would not be too wrong if silence were no more than absence of all noise and clamor. If deadly hush is all that is required to stimulate an atmosphere of inner calm and recollection, then every site, where death rules as an undisputed master, would be the legendary hunting ground for its ideal possession.

Yet as we know so well, this is not true. Silence is not a subject for the dead — dead in mind or dead in body — but it is forever the greatest challenge for the man who is alive. Death is, no doubt, efficient in its teaching on so many matters, but in this vital subject we gladly choose another master. All death can show us is the inability to speak, but it can never teach us silence. It mutes our tongues and seals our lips, it shuts our eyes and stops the rush of our thoughts, but are these the signs we are looking for? Is there not much more behind our search and expectations than the stillness which comes from lips which ceased to live? True silence is born in our hearts. Here, in the heart, lies the cradle of our virtue, as here in the heart lies the cause of its death: "Use all thy watchfulness to keep thy heart true; that is the fountain whence life springs." [1] If silent tongues alone accompany our solitude, we share our stillness with the beasts; but if we search into the depths of our soul, our calm and peace are shared by God himself.

Silence reveals the countenance of man by laying bare the very roots from where his depths are born. It has been said that men with a real message are quite rare but those who want to listen are still rarer. If that is true, we can not claim a laurel; since, unless we learn to listen, we will never grow, and if we stop growing, we soon will do no more than stress the obvious. No wonder that so many men who have ideas and wisdom flee into silence more than men of action, convinced as they must be, that the intensity of mind is not discovered by a show of shrewd performances or clever movements of the hands, but by an inner growth which hardly can be measured or be seen. Alone they wish to be with their own secret dreams, surrounded only by the stillness of their thoughts and in this favorable climate they steadily advance in their discoveries until they reach the point — the long desired point — when they are able to proclaim a truth which never was proclaimed before. Were not so many things discovered and invented by "men of a few words?" To put the greatest amount of thought into the smallest amount of words is not so often practiced as its opposite, but it is realized enough to make our culture prosper and advance. As every golden harvest needs the long hush of a deep, white winter, so do ideas need months or years for their maturity and bloom. If we tried to speed this growth with loud demands and noisy gestures, we only would destroy the gentle

[1] Prov. 4. 23.

88

climate which ideas require to prosper and to flourish: "A man may be the wiser for remaining dumb, where the glib talker grows wearisome; the silent man, has he nothing to say? Or is he waiting for the right time to say it? Wisdom keeps its utterance in reserve, where the fool's vanity can not wait. The babbler cuts his own throat." [2]

If our scientists in their relentless search for new discoveries desire to unveil more of the mysteries of our universe, they first must question silence and not speech. No sooner are our lips at rest, the soul of man awakens, ready to forge into this never ending stretch of land where secrets lay in wait to be at last detected and revealed. How often has one genial idea, with its identity revealed, served well the whole of our mankind.

Silence is fraught with elements of danger as it is often filled with disappointments and surprises. One never knows really what the unknown presents as its next move, nor are we ourselves in a position to presage the strategy with which we hope to checkmate our challenge. At times we must hold back our powers, as nature holds its breath before a storm; at other times we have to use our silence like a shout, as Christ used it when he refused to answer Herod. Yet, whatever shape our silence will assume, it will forever be the trademark of the strong. A weakling can not hold his tongue. He might profusely speak when he ought to keep silence and he might keep silence when he ought to speak. To learn to be attached to neither is just a little bit too much for his conceit and understanding. To talk for the sake of talking, this is the best use he can perceive for the tremendous gift of speech. If he is finally exhausted on the battlefield of his own words, he gladly seeks relief in all the noise of others: "Meanwhile they learn habits of idleness as they go from house to house; nor are they merely idle, they gossip and interfere and say what they have no right to say." [3]

It would be wrong now to conclude that silence exists in our life for its own sake. Such an exalted position it has never held. It is not even NATURAL for us, who are forever analyzed and registered as humans with a social need. We derive genuine pleasure in meeting our friends and neighbors and

[2] Ecclus. 20. 5–8.
[3] 1 Tim. 5. 13.

nothing could be more exciting than a spirited exchange of thoughts. We even like to hear our own voice and some consider this the loveliest sound they know. Do not all of us seek occasions to express our innermost desires and discuss our dreams with those noble enough to share them? Were we not ourselves helped so often by words of true encouragement and understanding? Speech surely can not be a bad thing, as a check on speech must be a good thing, and both perhaps together are the best thing which could happen to our daily export of conversations. But who is going to provide this check on our speech if not the valiant strength of our silence?

To treasure silence in its full impact and its power is to use it properly by making the most of all its values and its disciplines. Its inner strength can tame a speech into maturity and measure, while its inherent discipline conditions our flighty mind for serious thinking about the problems yet to solve. Those who are afraid of silence are often afraid of themselves, as those who flee from it flee from their own name. They hate to see their face reflected clearly in a mirror, so must confusion serve to guide their clumsy path. A blue sky has no doubt its beautiful attraction, but they who trot in heavy fog prefer a set of clouds and heavy drizzle: "Fools break out into rash utterance, where the prudent are at pains to weigh their words; with the one, to think is to speak, with the other, to speak is to think." [4]

Silence is not only a vital condition for the growth and development of inner values and greater depths; it it is also the beginning of those finer steps which ultimately lead to contemplation. Inner stillness quiets the pretentious voice of all the creatures and rests the mighty storms of our sea, so that, at last, our soul and its desires have found a welcomed change to make their wishes heard and understood. Years later — it might mean many years later — when contemplation reaches unexpected heights, silence is not only its well paid guardian but its supreme expression and its most blessed language. The poets and the artists need its hallowed possession as much as religious and priests: "Sleepless that thought holds me, yet bewildered and dumb. I reflect upon days long past, the immemorial years possess my mind; deep mus-

[4] Ecclus. 21. 28–29.

ings occupy my thoughts at midnight, never will my mind be at rest." [5]

How can we ever reach this peaceful state of mind or take possession of all these islands which allure us with their attractive calm and rest? Are we not chasing a wishful dream, never sure that we are able to span the breadth of its heavenly wings? Exterior silence is, no doubt, a help without which we perform but little. If it is considered lightly and discharged without respect, contemplation is crudely stifled in its growth and beauty. The brutal noise of our streets will rob it of its tender veil, while the subtle din of our hearts will ruin it in its very roots. The heart, may we never forget, is the more dangerous of the two. A public square can never raise the clamor which our heart is able to contrive. Put under stress of deep emotions, as love and fear can only fashion, our mind becomes so loud and restless that even a city full of strife and clatter is easier to endure. One driving passion creates a greater uproar in the hidden chambers of the soul than all the piercing rattle of a tense metropolis. When a disturbance comes from the din of our streets, the turmoil is but transitory and bound to disappear in proper moments, but if the heart is at the center of the howl, our soul is so deeply shaken and perturbed that it might take some years until the wound begins to heal: "Who dares climb the mountain of the Lord, and appear in his sanctuary? The guiltless in act, the pure in heart; one who never set his heart on lying tales, or swore treacherously to his neighbor." [6]

To clear the path for silence to gain its right position, we have to cleanse the walls of our hearts from all affections which are clearly wrong. In state of war with ourselves, we can never sign a peace agreement. If we try to serve two masters, we will only serve ourself. If our love is selfless, our heart is bound to be in peace, but if our affections are a lie, our soul will revolt against its chains. How deeply did Augustine experience the impact of this truth, when he sat down and wrote: "Instead I foamed in my wickedness, following the rushing of my own tide, leaving you and going beyond all your laws. Nor did I

[5] Ps. 76. 5–7.
[6] Ps. 23. 3–5.

91

escape your scourges. No mortal can. You were always by me, mercifully hard upon me and besprinkling all my illicit pleasures with certain elements of bitterness, to draw me on to seek for pleasures in which no bitterness should be." [7] Augustine left us long ago, but as his last will and testament he bequeathed us his eternal struggle and much of all the bitterness he tasted is still on our lips today. May we never cease to learn from him not only how he kindled the flame of his bitter lust but how he conquered his wily passions with the triumphant force of his indomitable faith.

Our century, which calls itself the greatest of them all, is basically absorbed and dedicated to the myth of action. Production rules our nation and "more production" is the dream which rules the little man on our street. Values which can not be seen or measured are treated with distrust and skepticism, whereas material profits are assessed with the highest ratings of the year. No wonder that silence and contemplation are treated like two little orphans, whom really no one wishes to adopt. Yet since they arrived and plan to stay, so they argue in their cold politeness, they must be made subservient to action, or they will lose the little reputation they still possess in the tiny realm which is yet their own. How can our ruthless race for "better living" afford the luxury of standing still? How can we gaze at the heavens above without taking away our eyes from the never resting line of mass production? Might not the man who flees into the world of silence miss his important turn in the assembly hall? Can hours missed at work ever return by work in our inner search for peace? Besides, another danger looms on the horizon, a danger which must be avoided at the cost of any price. If contemplation is allowed to choose its proper climate and grow on its own soil, it easily may lead beyond the natural horizons and lead us to a world which is as strange to us as God.

To ease the threat of all objections of activity, we can assert that the dynamics of our inner values are not so dangerous as our pragmatists believe, nor is it quite as simple as our modern agnostics might presume it is. Inner peace and contemplation never declared war on action, nor is it true that silence thrives on the destruction of all noise. Contemplation and

[7] Conf. 2. 2.

activity need each other as both are needed to make our society as perfect as we can make it. Activity, born on the depths of contemplation is action at its best, while contemplation interrupted by activity finds its most blessed balance. Where the small of mind find only shadows, the great of heart detect the light.

To practice silence one needs prudence. If we consider calmly all we must know, foresee and understand in order to act in prudence, we readily can understand that this specific gift is always in such great demand yet short forever in supply. How often we were eager and prepared to utter our views and judgments, yet prudence did suggest to seal our lips and keep the wisdom inside the fences of our heart. Fleeting words, uttered without due reflection, have not rarely caused a greater damage than wind-packed storms of hail and ice. We regretted perhaps the wounds we caused, but often these regrets came late. On the contrary, how many times have we escaped anxieties and fears because we knew the golden rule of silence and kept it. Prudence can be so exquisite and our friends so sensitive that we must be constantly alert and watchful lest we offend or violate the sacred rights which God has given to us all: "No such peril to a city as a great talker; for his rash utterance, no man so well hated as he." [8]

We owe silence to ourselves as much as we owe it to all others. With the same insight as we treat the special needs of our soul we have to attend to the need of those we love so much and those who love us so little. The inner capacity and strength of our tranquillity and calm must be so vigorous and wide that we shall never fail to understand and feel the stillness in the souls of others. To respect their privacy as we respect the sanctity of the house of God is only part of the price we pay for being human. One should not stress too much the old saying that love seeks knowledge of the secrets of the beloved, since this might lead us swiftly to the point of poor familiarity and boredom. To know all and everything means, far too often, to know too much. Love is so tender a gift from heaven that we should respect its loneliness and grandeur and not begin to violate its reticence and beauty with our clumsy questions or our senseless talk. Secrecy and inner calm are treasured as important parts of our personality and if one

[8] Ecclus. 9. 25.

forces his loud curiosity into our inner peace, he should be carelessly dismissed as an intruder. A person will remain a person in his full charm and vigor if he can keep his own account of secrets, and such a person will always present to us a challenge as long as he preserves the solitude he needs for his salvation. It is a privilege, reserved to God alone, to know ALL triumphs and defeats, while we poor humans, ugly sinners ourselves, should be content to know only as much as we need, to be of help to others. To force a secret to reveal itself is not so daring a performance as we may think, especially not in the case when our victim is distressed and totally abandoned. Perhaps he needs far greater strength and understanding to heal a wound than to open it. Much more is destroyed in man by use of force and violence than what is built up by silence and compassion: "Keep clear of quarreling and sin shall less abound. Quick temper sets feuds a-raging and wicked men there are that will embroil fast friends, and stir up strife among folk that lived in peace." [9]

The bitter failure to honor and respect the solitude of others can often reflect a deep contempt one has for his own soul and God. Is it purely a coincidence that modern atheism has invented all the gloomy wiles which force a man to break his silence and to confess against his better knowledge? Communism, in its perversity and pride, refuses to accept a sign of contradiction and if it senses contradiction in the making, it swiftly breaks it before it can speak. Communists prefer to subdue rebellious minds with pills and needles before they accept defiance from a will still free to resist. Are they perhaps afraid of silence because it spells so loudly their doom? Or are they fighting the eternal silence, which they claim does not exist, as their last hurdle on their road to hell? Or are they fighting just themselves, realizing that they themselves are their worst enemies? "Vanished away thy enemies, Lord, vanished away, and all their busy wickedness scattered to the winds!" [10]

Faithful silence keeps us company until our life has reached its fullness. It shares with us, since the beginning of all time all our torments, pains and sufferings and never has it begged for a reward. It has such a charming way of assuming our deepest self

[9] Ecclus. 28. 11.
[10] Ps. 91. 10.

with such perfection that it succeeds in freeing us even from the threats of anger and despair. No man has ever walked away from silence without having first been saved by it. Silence has so many names and presents so many worlds; it speaks for thoughts of many minds and shields religious of all nations. Yet as different as silence may be, it is always the same revelation, the same expression of the one silence, the one beyond, which came into our midst in a night which was so still and holy. Of this ONE silence — which was the WORD — all other silences are a reflection, hoping only to return again to their eternal source, which has no end and no beginning.

May we never say so much on earth that we are found speechless the very moment we have to explain to God, who we really are.

TWELVE

Not From Pleasures Alone

A brilliant mind embedded in a disciplined character can often read and interpret the signs of his own civilization. Warned perhaps or driven by an inner sight, such a man can clearly perceive the heights and depths of the prevailing culture and he has no fear to pronounce its hidden message. Not only centuries past have had their prophets who served their nations well through all the storms and battles; our times too are blessed with great intellects who understand the writings on the wall. With embarrassing clarity they often flash on our sullen minds the pictures we impress on history, and in exacting words they tell us what we suspected in our hungry, disappointed souls. As seers do they fathom the expressions of the hidden face of the tomorrow, and with the zeal of the old sages they cast their fury over our deeds of shame and fear. Applause does not affect their judgment, as ridicule will never change their mind. They only burn with the desire to proclaim the truth as they perceive it in their harassed soul. In favor or disgraced, accepted or banned, their voice will never die. It dwells in our midst as our cherished blessing or our cursed damnation.

Prophets never die; they only change. Our kind of messenger is not exactly like his antique counterpart, but true and fear-

less just the same. He clipped some of the wings which our fore-
bears pinned on all the clouds of heaven, not to believe less, but
to strengthen the roots of our honored faith. He shaved his beard
and cooled the fire in his eyes not to be less impressive or majestic, but to be more like the man who preached the sermon on
the mount. Even the thunder in his fateful voice has mellowed to
let the power of persuasion be stronger than the fear of punishment. One thing, however, he did not change — the message itself. What he proclaims today is just as much of a caution to us
as it was to the trembling Jews when bearded Moses thundered
at them in the lonely deserts and in the abandoned mountains.

As a nation we are warned today that we have sold our hearts
to pleasures. We created an image which is not gravitating towards the eternal power of ideas, but shifting decisively towards
the soft attraction which pleasures exert on the feeble will of
man. Our particular time in history is deeply implicated by the
rapacious drive of our hungry instincts and marked forever by
the incessant gratification of our craving appetites. We have
stigmatized our own age as the black market of all perverse and
hollow pleasures. If we were asked today by our friends or enemies to translate our most intimate aspirations into one short
and understandable sentence, we could swiftly reply — more
pleasures. Love of entertainment and an ever-increasing hunger
for amusements make up the pages of the gospel which we
preach from our billboards and advertise in our color-maga-
zines and journals. With the supermarkets as our new civilization
centers and our dull and repetitious commercials as our blessed
hymns, we offer to the searching nations of today a philosophy of
life which is so flat and empty that no one is tempted to pay serious attention to its hollow message. Even for the poorest, it is too
cheap to buy. Do not vast empires of our industries work without interruption to produce for our people not what they really
need but what they wish and want? Popular fancy and the whim
of the crowds rule the wheels of our gigantic production and if
these whims are getting tired, they are swiftly excited again by
greater floods of boisterous commercials. Like deadened sheep the
multitudes become alerted again by all the songs of newer jingles
and rush to buy what they are told they must possess to live. No

wonder that we do not hesitate to pour more money into the oily throat of advertising than into the vital issue of education. Our youth seems to be outgraded in importance by our signposts on the highways: "Fatal path, that ensnares the reckless! Pitiful end of the men that love life! There they lie in the world beneath, huddled like sheep, with death for their shepherd, the just for their masters; soon, soon their image fades, the grave for its tenement." [1]

Once we were known as a nation of courage. Today our skin has softened to a point where we are not taken too seriously any more by our friends or enemies. Being always challenged by the power of a purpose, we realize all of a sudden that the purpose has abandoned us and left us stranded in the battle for the mind of man. Like a beggar who was once a king, we still fight for a leading place amongst the nations proclaiming to possess the highest standard of good living and a record output in production, knowing, however, so well that private consumption is not the ultimate aim of life.

Pleasure favors weakness, never strength. A strong, disciplined soldier is prepared to endure hardships and privations for an extended period of time, whereas the enfeebled man has to rush back to the elusive fountains of excitements and of gratifications to stimulate again his waning energies. To preserve the warmth of our cozy corners and to prolong the hours of our playful laughters, this is the call and the ideal which fascinates the hearts of a substantial segment of the population. To push forward into the unknown or to hunt down the ruthless enemies and face the grim and deadly battle, this is the noble task of television and the heroes of the movies. The ever-patient screen revives in living color the ideal which once before was our inspiration, but which is buried now in our stately graveyards. If we judge ourselves these days, we still consider ourselves proud citizens of the strongest nation in the world, forgetting however the tragic connection which exists between the sudden fall of nations and their lack of a higher purpose. No wonder that our national mood prefers to be defensive rather than offensive.

A sensual civilization such as ours has no determined form or

[1] Ps. 48. 14–15.

shape. As anything else which originates from pleasure, it defies exacting rules and definitions. We forbid ourselves the right
to draw limits, nor do we accept boundaries which we promise
never to overstep again. Freedom in the choice of pleasures is
the only law we know. Almost anything which pleases our senses
is allowed today and freely served to our youth, which pays a
bitter price for our folly. Moral values are distorted and glamorous crimes presented as a worthwhile challenge. Purity and
heroism are golden relics of another age and steadily replaced
by the image of the moral degenerate who is entitled to his
piece of "self-expression." Should doubts and questions arise in
our sleepy conscience which could stir up the sense of guilt, we
quickly relegate "these problems" to the busy doctor and to
the healing touch of the psychiatrist. Since good and evil are
only a sort of chemical battle in the veins of the individual, let
the doctors decide what is conducive to the peace of our soul
and let them prescribe the pills to be taken to combat our sins and
our passions. If unrest perseveres however and problems stay awake
at night, we swiftly rush to our modern books which serve so readily
the newest non-religious answer to a purely-religious question.
Should, however, all these "techniques" fail to produce the inner
harmony and peace, then the miraculous barbiturates, sold in millions, will neutralize the troublemakers and soothe the waves of the
ruffled sea, at least for a few hours.

No wonder that our pleasure-based materialism, with no
deeper ideas in its marrow, is not much of a match for the ideol-
ogy of our cunning foes. While our outlook on life is purely
pragmatic and commercial, their dialectic materialism is founded
on deep ideas requesting discipline and obedience from its disciples, even stretching to the point of rendering one's life for the
sake of the community. Perhaps the hardened Christian in a com-
munist-dominated country has to accept a greater challenge to his
faith than we in our self-indulgent West. Behind the borders of
extinguished freedom the Christian has to count on sufferings and
even martyrdom for his convictions, whereas we in our land of
liberty and faith can only lose the chains of riches and prosperity.
In the end the message of Christ may be just as embarrassing to
us as it is to the mind of the confused communists. Some even as-

sert, and may they be wrong, that it causes greater consternation to the Christian West than to the atheistic East.

Love of pleasures, humanity's ancient passion, is something which accompanies human nature all the time. Yet there is a vast difference between the ancient slavery to sensual passions and the modern frenzy for unrestrained self-expression. The sensuality of our modern age does not stem from the idea that such a pleasure is an end desirable in itself, as the ancients believed. Our drive for pleasures originates in the worship of the human mind, which chooses to be its own law and its undisputed master. Behind the wildest passions of today is the ugly shout of the apostate who surrendered his faith to the whims of his instincts. The modern renegade, staggering in his own morass, knows so well what his religion teaches and requests, but he refuses to listen to any command but his own. Abandoned by the challenge from beyond, he makes the most of all that this earth can seduce him to enjoy: "True it is, wise men die; but reckless fools perish no less; their riches will go to others, and the grave will be their everlasting home. Age after age, they will live on there, under the fields they once called their own. Short is man's enjoyment of earthly goods; match him with the brute beasts, and he is no better than they." [2] While the ancient pagans could afford to vegetate like happy animals, the modern apostate will always remain haunted by the memory of God, who refused to be forgotten. No wonder that our modern philosophies are only an outcry of human loneliness and hopeless despair. Can anyone be more abandoned than a man who lost his God and can not find himself? Such a man creates again the fatal night into which Judas fled after he betrayed his master. One sold his Lord for money, the other for what money can buy. Is there any difference?

It would be unwise to conclude now that the only way to salvage this situation is to forbid our hearts to laugh. No one in our midst intends to put a cloak of suspicion on our joys and jubilations, nor are we asked to close the sources of our blessed relaxations. To do that would be sheer fanaticism, and even virtue, as we know so well, can easily be miscast. The notion

[2] Ps. 48. 11–13.

that even our legitimate desires must be frustrated is not always safe. Some might be tempted to declare an attitude like that as "holy," forgetting however that our Lord did not put us on this earth to make our lives miserable, but to work out our eternal happiness with joy and enthusiasm. Deliberate denials, good as they may be, are of little value unless they help us to fulfill much better God's holy will on earth. Pleasures, therefore, as any other helpful means which leads to a higher end, are an important factor in establishing the much-desired balance in our tense and hasty life. Yet they must remain a means and never assume the commanding position of an "end in itself." Monopoly of pleasures is the cursed situation we deplore. To live for pleasures alone and to forget everything else, this is the poisonous weed which kills the flowers in the gardens. To see on the skies nothing but the glittering stars of our entertainers is just as wrong as to see there only threatening clouds of sorrows and calamities. Balance is the golden key to our peace of soul. Yet this necessary balance is never to be achieved, as long as the weight of all the pleasures tips too heavily on our scales: "Joy to you in the Lord at all times; once again I wish you joy. Give proof to all of your courtesy. The Lord is near. Nothing must make you anxious." St. Paul, who wrote these precious lines, was a man with a great mission in his stormy soul. He dreamed to subject all the borders of the universe to the gentle reign of his triumphant Saviour. Strained as he must have been for leisure, he fully realized that without joy in our hearts we are not to be counted amongst the true disciples of a Master who was so pleased to attend a wedding feast and who made sure that the guests had enough wine to drink.

There is today in our land an urgent need of moral disciplines and spiritual transformation. If we desire to recapture some of the idealism which made us so famous in history, we have to tame the beast in our instincts, so that the mighty power of the mind can rule again the fate of our nation. Restraint and firmness in our homes and in the realms of public life will serve us well in the titanic struggle of survival. To be the richest nation in this world should never satisfy our dreams; to become the most daring and triumphant one, THIS should excel as our challenge.

It is not too late yet in the hour of our fate. Nations without God have never existed and we can be sure our epoch is no exception to this rule. Too many corners of our magnificent planet show the footprints of its maker, and there are always enough men and women who know how to read. Our land is not different. In spite of all the floods of pleasures which overflow the gutters of the streets, there always are those who are too good for headlines. Fortitude and courage still grow strong in the roots of our soil. Our hearts are not only bursting with tranquilizers and barbiturates; they also harbor fearless faith, so strong at times that it can move a mountain. As hardly any other nation, we freely admit our guilt, and blame no one else for the block we stumble on. Conscious that the weed in our garden was planted by our own seed, we do not refuse to accept the harvest. What has happened to us, we know we deserved. Just like the good thief on the cross, we readily confess with often heart-rending sincerity that the punishment we suffered was not unjust: "And one of the two thieves who hung there fell to blaspheming against him; Save thyself, he said, and us too, if thou art the Christ. But the other rebuked him; What, he said, hast thou no fear of God, when thou art undergoing the same sentence? And we justly enough; we receive no more than the due reward of our deeds." [3]

Doom is not imminent, nor are there nightmares on the way to nest. Hope as a virtue and as a stark reality still determines strongly the climate and the mood of our nation. We have yet to surrender, and whoever expects us to do so will be in for a surprise. Treasures of hidden gold can still be mined from the hearts of our best. The sins of our pleasures, great as they may be, will never outgrow the power of our holy faith. More than anything else, it is this faith which we claim as our heritage. If we are shy a bit, or even reluctant to project the depths of our faith more into the open, as other nations prefer to do, it is not due to lack of generosity or kindness, but due to the deep conviction that if we love God sincerely enough we do not need to force this love unto our lips nor into our gestures. To put a tender veil on the secret of our souls and to let our deeds speak

[3] Luke 23. 39–41.

102

rather than our lips, this is more to our liking. War-torn Europe in its ghastly ruins and its piercing hunger has proved with its glorious resurrection that our faith and our help were real and blessed. Other nations perhaps are more talented to speak scholarly about God and his mysteries, but if it comes to the point to prove our love in action, we always wish to be counted amongst the first. We at least hope that our Lord may be pleased with all we try to DO for him, and perhaps our deeds may be just as pleasing to his countenance as all the learned books of others.

A long road is stretched out before our weary eyes, a road infested with bursting dangers and tremendous glories. To walk it is our duty, and never to escape from it is our solemn promise. Many a wound, which our own folly has inflicted on us, has to heal first before we can be acclaimed again as the triumphant leader of tomorrow. Yet, may we never forget that it is impossible to change the fibre of our nation or reverse its moral character unless we clean our own souls first. If we continue to submerge ourselves in the never-ending stream of pleasures, while others are drowning in the waves of hunger, we not only are unjust to others but also take a risk, that terrible risk, that God may decide to save the hungry and let us perish.

THIRTEEN

My Gift To You

A man who freely states that he has never offered help to anyone or confesses without embarrassment that he was never asked
for help, such a man is a violent contradiction of every wish
and desire which God in his compassionate love has imprinted
on our immortal souls. If a man like that exists, he lives on a
level which is not only inhuman, but almost below the level
of our untamed beasts. In his soul he has debased himself to
a degree which we find rarely in our busy midst. It is almost a
part of the human instinct to rush to the aid of the needy,
stretch out our hands to raise again the fallen to his feet. It
brings comfort and joy to us to let others make use of our
strength and lend them the force of our courage. As much as
we need air to breathe, so much does our soul need the indi-
gence and sorrow of others to grow, deepen and clarify. To
drain back all our love and all our desires into our own blood
stream, and kiss forever our own success, makes the land of our
soul dwindle so swiftly into a barren and dreary desert.

The climate of our times has inspired the heart of man with
a significant and far-reaching desire for unity. The demand to
unite is heard so often today that its message overshadows every

other piece of news in our papers. Unity turns more and more into the great hope of mankind, to avoid perhaps a terrible catastrophe which could annihilate the center of our universe. Instead of destroying everything, we still can choose the other alternative, uniting everything. Not at the expense of eternal truth, as some are inclined to suggest, but at the expense of intense hatred and partial love. Narrowness of mind and jealousy of heart are gradually losing their grip. The dividing lines which have separated one from the other are broken down to make space for a bridge which can link the various islands to one powerful stretch of land. Countries which looked at each other with envy and hostility are ready today to unite their markets and plow away their stretch of boundaries. Races of different shades of skin, who hated to share the very breath of air, begin to grasp their different anxieties, and are trying to unite their souls which are beyond the reach of any color. Hearts of different faith commence to leave behind their old and long suspicions and try again to love each other as our Lord requested two thousand years ago. This very moment the most illustrious minds in our midst are praying to the almighty and eternal Truth to find the blessed way again which leads us back to the hill on which our Lord has died for all of us. "It is not only for them that I pray; I pray for those who are to find faith in me through their word; that they may all be one; that they too may be one in us, as thou, father, art in me, and I in thee." [1] While there exists no heated dispute about the necessity of union, there are some deep and bitter disagreements about the way to bring this precious dream into existence. Some believe that naked force will beat the heart into submission, while others rely on cunning threats and sweet reprisals. The great ones, however, aim to achieve the precious unity with the unselfish help they can offer to those who hunger and thirst after far more than food and drink can offer. "Whatever gifts are worth having, whatever endowments are perfect of their kind, these come to us from above; they are sent down by the father of all that gives light; with whom there can be no change, no swerving from his course." [2]

[1] John 17. 20–21.
[2] James 1. 17–18.

To help is an art which some learn well, while others never seem to graduate. Who is the student who rates the highest in these elements and what are the talents he must possess to become a master in this venture?

He must show INTEREST in others. If he WANTS to help others, he will be of help, but if he has the cold and measured attitude of "self-love" he will surely fail, even if his egotism is very cleverly covered up and deeply hidden. The needy man has not only his hunger sharpened, but with the hunger his inner sense of sincerity and truthfulness. It is not hard for him to distinguish the disguise from the real. If I cherish the secret attitude "I really am not concerned about what happens to others," my flimsy help becomes a lie and never turns into the gracious blessings of a gift. Something in man must appeal to my heart, something far greater than an important name or exciting beauty or the clumsy weight of gold and silver, and this something is the exalted knowledge that the hidden face of Christ looks at me in the man I am destined to meet. If I never learn to unravel this hidden face of Christ from the greedy mud and lustful mire, I will always remain a poor and shabby friend, who runs away from poverty and sickness, and hides from ugliness and threats of persecution. From the shores of my life I have to build a lofty bridge into the land of the next one; otherwise, I will never meet the man who is so anxiously waiting for my arrival. Some of us seem to possess a special charisma in dealing with others, and they are to be envied since a charisma can never be learned. Their natural ability, deepened perhaps with serious studies, makes them the born leaders in the tensions and the storms of life. To count such a man amongst the number of my friends is a blessing of its own. If every one else is tempted to abandon me, he will always remain at my side, offering me his precious aid the very moment when I did not expect help anymore.

The greater my sensitivity, the more effective will be my contribution. I have to be able to experience in my heart the feelings of others and understand the seeming lack of them. To tune into another one's wave length and to receive its secret message is the sign of a mature and noble mind. One has to possess great inner strength if one can truly say, "I know what you are going through, and I sense so deeply how much you were hurt." Those, of course, who suffered in their own domain will always have a deeper reach than the man who plays the lucky clown through all his life.

A specialty of a few — I wish I would be amongst them — is to discern and understand the things which the other did not mention but hid from the knowledge and the sight of man. Those who come to us to look for help use so often their fluent wordiness to test our own inner bearings. Their real intentions are, at first, well covered and not at all brought into the open. If we can read the inner writings of a soul without any exterior clue, we capture not only the imaginations of our needy friends but also the precious love of their grateful hearts.

There are, however, situations in life, perhaps moments of intense afflictions, when the best help we can offer is our loving silence. Pains and sufferings can reach depths in the human soul which go beyond the sphere of our lips. A word would only hurt; however, my silent presence is a golden blessing. We have to feel such delicate situations, and while they occur on rare occasions, they do, however, exist. The man who is interiorly free possesses the best geiger-counter for such a silent beat of heart; the man who is upset in his own heart can never fathom silence. How can we grasp and endure the storms of others if our own shores are ravaged by the tempest of our greed and passions.

In order to develop and to perfect our inner sensitivity, we must study many lessons and learn from books which tell us more about the inner world of our heart. The best instructor, however, who can teach us will always be the creature MAN himself. Man can teach us what no ink has ever written. Those who love us and those who oppose us can test our knowledge to its very marrow and reveal to us the worth of our wisdom. Especially the unsympathetic pupil, the man I never liked, is prone to become the object of my greatest success. To love a man, whom I do not like, is next to the impossible, and few there are in our midst who claim a title to this triumph.

To make God's order "love your enemies" come more and more to life, we have to remember that not everything which looks like malice stems from malice. We know so little about the reasons why a man becomes irresponsible and wicked. He might be made of the same fibre as we are, but we succeeded in our efforts, whereas he had the misfortune to fail and lose in his endeavors. The terrible pangs of loneliness and uselessness might never cease to hunt his steps, whereas we are happy and content with our family and our friends. Inner sufferings and sickness of which we have so little knowledge, and which we ourselves never had to endure, are perhaps a constant threat to this man's safety and rob him of his peace and joy. Injustices, at last, which fate has never laid on our shoulders, have followed this man's step so long that he waits only for the hour of revenge. It is quite easy to tell a man that he is bad, but it is so hard to tell him why! The gifted artist who looks through the mask and reaches the secret wounds can be immensely helpful; the amateur who only perceives the mask will swiftly flee from its frightening grimace and secure his safety first. No doubt to help a benevolent friend brings joy and pleasure, but to rush to the aid of an enemy is so difficult and rare that the surprise of it may even be felt in heaven. To keep the gate of our heart wide open while another tries so hard to shut it is so remarkable an achievement that it can hardly be accounted for by human strength alone. The grace from the heavens above has to come to our urgent assistance and confer on our timid souls the courage and the wisdom to overcome our inner resistance and perform this earthly wonder: "If you love those who love you, what title have you to a reward? Will not the publicans do as much? If you greet none but your brethren what are you doing more than others? Will not the very heathen do as much?" [3]

Next to sensitivity, a certain modest reserve is advantageous in helping a soul to find its inner freedom and its peace. The hands which offer help should not become oppressive nor so clumsy that our gifts turn into burdens of embarrassment. To step to the beloved sidelines, which some seem always to forget, and guide from there the climb of our friends, reveals so great a mind that only few can claim its enviable possession. We know too well from long experience that many plant the seed for no other purpose but to indulge in the crop of the harvest. They re-

[3] Matt. 5. 46–47.

fuse to let the name of our Lord catch the glittering rays of attention, and they steal from the pockets of heaven a treasure which has never belonged to them. "What do we have which we did not receive," asked St. Paul, "And if we received it why do we glory in it?" What is of a personal nature in the stream of my life is probably more boring than I would like to admit, and often something looks quite impressive and majestic to the judgment of my own mind, while it appears rather trivial and pale to the appraisals of others. Thus it seems a rather safe rule of conduct to narrate less than more from the pages of my diary and to let the irresistible power of ideas substitute for my own personal glamour.

It is a real talent, which is not too widespread, to bring others to the precious point where they are willing to reveal their hearts and let us read the secret lines of their triumphs and defeats. It needs tremendous tact and generous nobility to accept and bear such confidence and not to betray this gentle gift of need and trust. To hear and not to hear, to feel and not to feel, to love and not to lose one's heart, these are the demands and tensions which a great apostle has to tame in his own inner world. The man who accepts this challenge is on his way to become another redeemer in this begging world of ours. If we, however, are still irritated and perturbed by the "peculiarities" of man, we will not be of use in any needy situation. Impatiently we will serve answers which were so swiftly taken from a book but never tested by our hearts. God seems to love limitless variety and has plenty of room for endless differences, but we are forever tempted to press the whole world into our narrow frame.

Our help is most effective if we possess responsibility in our heart. If we realize that the gift we offer to another can bring eternal happiness to him or cursed damnation, we will think twice before we present our donation to the man who longs for it. Not many responsibilities are greater than the responsibility to help. The mechanism of the soul is so fine and tender that only trained specialists should approach this mysterious land. Even the slightest perturbance, injustice or simple oversight is able to upset the inner harmony of a person for many years to come. What damage can be caused by a man who is a fool without knowing it!

A determined harshness, or the cold climate of narrow zeal, or petty insistence on "our way of thinking" can paralyze the inner growth of hope and ruin the chances of a man for his entire span of life. It is so easy to declare a man's mentality as "over-sensitive." True as this statement may be, it brings, however, no solution to the man who suffers under this affliction and knows no means to conquer this distress.

The echo of our words can stretch as far as our hearts can reach. Our praise carries strength enough to build a world anew, where-as bitter criticism is destructive enough to burst apart a blooming harvest. Are we not helped much in our life by noble gestures of encouragement or words of approbation and of joy? Are we not hurt much by vicious floods of unkind judgments and reproaches? As we feel and as we react, so feels and reacts the man who is my neighbor. Let us remember that in times of war and peace.

One medicine, however, has never failed to cure the patient. It seems to be effective in every climate where it is used; "AC-TUAL HELP." The snow and ice in the land of my harshest opponents seem to melt away so swiftly, if I, without delay, ob-tain some aid in their behalf. Our help in deeds, and not in promises, is the only language no one fails to understand. Per-haps some of our adversaries grow suspicious of our preaching and do not like to listen any more to our pleas, since our words remain alone and die without an echo. Has not our Lord stressed the point that deeds will be counted in our last judgment, and not the number of sermons we delivered? It is not hard to preach a eulogy which is copied from the pages of a book, but to deliver proofs of our sincerity and holiness requests much more than ink and paper can reveal. Some, no doubt, possess a bril-liant fluency of speech whereas others enjoy the quiet gift of kindness and of love. Both are needed in the wholesome life of our rich society, since both have to maintain their rightful place in our land. May, however, the orator never grow so powerful in influence and might that the gracious virtues of our heart are talked to death and buried under a heap of hollow phrases.

At the end, a point might be mentioned which could easily turn our help into the most beautiful action of our whole life. Grace the person who is in need with the blessed chance to offer help to us. As poor as the beggar may look, he still possesses something which we can imitate and absorb. No one has everything, as no one has nothing. An icy front of strict perfection can easily be a lie which hides a weakness worse than poverty. To pretend to be beyond the reach of human help is to deny that all of us are beggars before the throne of the Almighty. Should not everyone in our midst be able to say, "What you told me last time was such a wonderful help to me. May God reward your kindness!"

Such a sentence revealed in earnest rings forth like a triumphant symphony in the heart of the destitute. He who never dared to believe to be of use to anyone suddenly learns the jubilant message that a word of HIS brought comfort and aid to a soul in need and distress. Victoriously he looks at the glittering stars of a contented heaven, free from fear and free of greed, for he knows now so clearly and deeply that he is not poor any more, but rich. "What you did to the least of your brethren, you have done to me."

FOURTEEN

Different Dimensions Of Life

In the never-ceasing struggle between the superior course of which the mind approves and the less noble path which the passions crave for, man has to be forever alert in his decisions, lest he fall prey to some desires of which he is embarrassed and ashamed. With the ability in his heart to embrace what he actually hates, and with the faculty in his soul to betray the ideals in which he firmly believes, he has to perform the work of his salvation in "fear and trembling," lest he become a party to the crime which he bewails and punishes. In the midst of enemies, assaulted on the right and on the left, he must heedfully chart his course so as to avoid the snares laid out by all the cunning of his nature and by the yearnings of his pride.

Though there is no man who can expect to be exempt from all hazards of this struggle, we differ greatly in the moment of our final count. Some come through in brilliant fashion, while others labor with a poor performance, and a few perhaps in our midst, pricked by strange anxieties and fears, keep no account at all, afraid they discover "zero" as their number. Yet, whatever the total sum of our final count will be, no passenger in this ship of life can claim a perfect record, since all of us have to admit that we failed and were defeated. We started out with high ideals of what had to be done and what had to be avoided, but these ideals have slowly undergone a change, like dreams we cherished, but which never saw the sun. At first there were the compromises, so quickly followed by adjustments and concessions, and then came the decisions, which surely hurt us the most, decisions against the warnings of our better knowledge. These we have made, not only once but often, and we will succumb to them as long as we are trying to stem the tide of our instincts. No wonder that bewilderment ensues from all the dissappointing scores of life, and it is not too strange to find our mind tempted with the thought to throw away the challenge of the ideal and lead a life according to the "least resistance." Why strive for peaks of mighty mountains when our valleys are so green? This tempting thought — as poisonous as any thought can be — lurks stubbornly behind the blinds of our character, ready to erupt at the propitious moment and proclaim itself the ruler of the mind. To hope that it will disappear or wither and never show its ugly face again is vain and useless. It surely will stay with us, and it will never starve, since it is nurtured and sustained by the most vital powers we possess.

We own life, this is true, but never as we own a book which written once never changes its face again. Life is a restless gift, forever turning like the mighty waves of our stormy oceans, jovial and gay with its friends of warmth and relaxation, tense and alarmed with its associates of terror and of fear. Living in these conflicting tensions is the creature MAN, who mirrors these gigantic flames of life in his relentless drive to create, in his fiery will to attain power, and in his fierce and often cruel determination to survive.

Man is proud to create. Never satisfied to copy or to imitate, never contented to borrow or to steal, but forever hunting the new image on the vast horizons of his soul, this is the highest aim the human genius can ever reach. To think what mind has never thought of, to build what never had been built before, to say a word which never crossed the lips of men, these are the human triumphs which only our best are destined to achieve. Being the center of his own existence, man projects into these creative forces his own talents and his skills, and he alone moulds inspirations to his proper name and personal approval. No two will ever be alike.

There is the man, the noblest perhaps of them all, who dares to set his challenge to the greatest height on earth — to recreate the life of the mightiest man who ever lived — Christ. Endowed with a rich, highly developed, interior life, and laboring at times under strong, powerful emotions, he challenges a force far greater than his own. Exultant joys and frightening depressions are only part of the stern expense he has to pay for his gallant and audacious adventure. A deep inner concentration requests from him a narrowing of other interests which can disturb the dialogue between the worlds so far apart, and yet so close together. Delights, innocent and fair, are often shunned and sacrificed for an allurement which is beyond the shores of our understanding. No wonder that even his friends are sometimes puzzled by his silence and angered by his speech, while enemies, who fail to understand the call from heaven, begin to hate and persecute the man who is too great for their bewildered judgment: "I have told you this, so that your faith may not be taken unawares. They will forbid you the synagogue; nay the time is coming when anyone who puts you to death will claim that he is performing an act of worship to God; such things they will do to you, because they have no knowledge of the Father or of me." [1]

There are masters amongst those men of courage as there are imitations which are quite poor and lifeless. None however has ever reached a greater height than Francis of Assisi. He created the finest masterpiece on earth. Convinced that God, the mysterious maker of the world, exists, he had but one desire left in his exalted soul: to herald and to proclaim, with all his might, the reign of Christ on earth. What he possessed, he sold, and what he could not sell, he gave away. Soon, not even a roof was left to keep the storms out of his cell. But neither rain nor any other threat of cold and bitter weather could dampen his enthusiasm for the beloved king of his own choice. St. Francis became the richest beggar who ever asked for a piece of bread. No wonder that "THEY" understood him not. Gradually the saint was forced

[1] John 16. 1–3.

to cut the wings of his exalted dream and level his hallowed message to the dull and listless ears of those who wished to follow him. The world loves the mediocre and pampers those whose mind is small. Confronted with real greatness, it has no answer left to give. St. Francis cried, but his tears helped him not; he suffered, but his sufferings were of no avail; he finally lost the sight of his eyes, so that in his blindness he could catch the dream again which was too great to become true.

Next to the saint, God placed the artist, whose powers to create are greater than the might of our seas and mountains. Unlike the saint, he does not wrestle with the force of God himself, but is content to struggle with ideas which emanate from God's tremendous greatness and mirror his eternal beauty. Filled in his heart with captivating visions, and pressed by urges of ever newer realizations, he is at times so far away from all the steps of our time that he seems awkward, if not quaint, to those who can not share his calling nor understand the meanings of his gifts. Like a saint, the artist finds strange loneliness his constant partner to success or failure. Creating his own inner world, in which his highly strung sensitivities find place to bloom and flourish, he twice becomes a stranger: once to himself and once to those who fail to appreciate his mission. There exists, however, a moment when all the agonies and tensions flee the artist and leave his heart in peace and joy — the precious moment of fulfillment. Confronted with his own achievements, praised by his brilliant monuments and immortal symphonies, the artist senses that the message entrusted to his care has been delivered. His duty is fulfilled. But until the moment arrives when he sees or touches his own piece of art, the world is only a wasteland, with him as a pilgrim . . . lost.

Next to the saint and near to the artist, God put the most beautiful piece of his work, the woman. To her the great privilege is given to create in flesh what others are destined to bring forth in spirit. As an echo to the voice of an angel, the woman was selected to bear not only Divinity but humanity as well. "Be it done unto me" was spoken not only once but time and again in Christian history, and through this greatest sentence ever uttered, the woman became a symbol of the spirit of total consecra-

115

tion to God and man. Her natural capacity for giving, paired with the desire to love others more than herself, became the basis for her glorious vocation on both sides of this universe. To rule this world by the might of our swords and missiles is to admit that we are weak, but to guide our lives and destinies with equity and love, this is the strength and calling of the woman who rules and governs our homes. Spiritually, as well as physically, the woman is the fountain and the nurturer of our life. The genius in man excels in works of arts and history; women leave their imprints on the masterpiece of life itself. Imbued with the conviction that life is sacred, she inspires man not to destroy the blooming harvest, but to guard the precious gift she bears. No wonder that in the life of many a great man we discover the influence of a noble woman, who through her inspiration and love brought the best in him to life. As long as she continues to fulfill her role in our destiny, not only our homes but also our nation will be strong and blessed.

Paired with the relentless drive to create is the forceful will of man to attain power. Man loves power. In its brutal appearance, when it demands the blood of others, it is the cursed pregorative of few, but in its gentle reign of influence for better, it is the privilege of many. A healthy society is one in which chances are given to leaders to emerge from all classes in the population, and within their spheres these leaders have the same responsibilities and duties as the heads of our governments. The masses alone do not accomplish much; they usually follow the call of the exceptional man, who not only possesses power, but knows how to put it to its most efficient use. As history proves, in our days especially, the genius of leadership seems as likely to flourish in some humble dwelling as in a mansion of wealth and influence. The number of luxuries we are able to enjoy does not reveal the number of talents a man calls his possessions. What marks the man of power and importance is sensitivity and insight, initiative and determination. There are no doubt the passive persons who are contented to enjoy this life through the gifts and help of others, and they forever wait until an action is forced on them by the determination of the stronger. They never sense the feel of power, nor do they mind to be an echo to the voice from other lips. Not that they are

116

mute, they can be very loud and noisy, but their noise is emptied of convictions and lacks the prominence of lively faith. For such, there is no need to aspire to places in front of others, since they do not know how to keep an exalted position. A sluggard or a coward will never learn to wear a crown.

The acceptance of HIGHER standards of judgment is the basis of sound power, as it is the best foundation of any progress we can hope to make in our civilization. High quality is the only quality a leader has to know. Short of a masterpiece, he never should lay aside his brush. Idealism — so scarce an item on our modern markets — is still the most trustworthy companion of real greatness. Once a leader has decided upon the part he has to play in life, he needs the stamina of courage and idealism to secure the final outcome of his mission. If idealism is banned from the desk of our rulers, brutality will take its place, and any nation which endures such an alternative without revolt deserves the bitter price it has to pay for such a folly.

The man of power who is set to rule must pay the debts of discipline. Not that we imply that he has to withdraw from the public squares and choose the desert as his roof, but it entails decisive moderation and control, wherever these are requested, to promote the ends he seeks. First in place means first in excellence. If he expects so much from others, others expect much more from him. It is not too surprising a fact that a large number of men who were destined to real greatness were men who learned first the art of obeying. Only after they learned how to take an order were they able to issue one. One without the other could easily create a tyrant whom we fear so much and love so little. Has not the most powerful man whoever lived in our world said: "I came to serve and not to be served."

A man of influence is not allowed to take his laurels home and rest. Born to stay ahead, he has to keep his dreams and his imagination alive, even at the price of his own peace and comfort. The moment he only watches new trends from a distance, he is losing his drive and importance. If he stays alert, however, in the midst of great contention, success will not abandon him. To set up new procedures and linger lazily to see them work, this is a luxury a man of power is not able to afford. Routine weakens

117

the toughest fibres, and few there are who can resist its sweet embrace. To ride the waves and not to cause them is a sign that men have lost their force and power. The real enthusiasm never fails to stimulate new energies, which in return produce another harvest.

Real power and its bearing will vary with the talents we received: "So it was with a man who went on his travels; he called his trusted servants to him and committed his money to their charge. He gave five talents to one, two to another, and one to another, according to their several abilities, and with that he set out on his journey." [2] We are not classified by our master as better because we have received a higher portion of those talents, nor are we of less interest to him because the quantity of our abilities is insignificant and small. What is of bearing in the mind and heart of our judge and maker is how we multiplied the gifts we have accepted. The profits we procured in God's eternal interest are weighed and counted on the sheet of our final tally. If I was foolish enough to dig a hole into the barren ground and bury there forever the powers which God entrusted to my solicitude, I will be cast into a darkness where there shall be weeping and gnashing of teeth. But if I accepted the challenge of this never-settled world of ours and executed well my strategies and missions, if I defied the nagging little voices of selfishness and envy and brought new life to hunger and despair, then I can report with joy in my exalted heart: "Lord it was five talents thou gavest me, see how I have made a profit of five talents besides."

Creation and power are forever linked to the grim and fiery struggle to survive. Like the most cunning of all animals, man senses the trap of his extinction and leaps into security with a speed and sureness which are not only stunning and superb, but frightening as well and cruel. Man hates to be annihilated. He loves to live and cleaves to this elusive gift with a fury which is so fierce and threatening that it can bend at times the gates of iron and of steel. To surrender life is the last thing on earth man is willing to surrender. Only the mind in darkness is prone to destroy with its own breath the vital flame of his existence. The man

[2] Matt. 25. 14–16.

118

in full command of all his senses will only use his powers to protect and to defend what is as holy to him as his own faith.

Life is my responsibility. I can not negotiate it at any public market, nor can I auction it off to any higher bidder. God alone, who was mighty enough to bestow it on us, is strong enough to take it, and he will do so at the moment known to him from all eternity. Until that moment strikes on the bell of life, I must lead this life, develop it, and bring it to a height which mirrors all the talents I possess. Not extra-ordinary means are requested to keep my health at proper level, but means at my good reach must be employed to foster and secure my body's strength and valor. It is equally foolish to fail through "too-much" as to do harm through "too-little." The golden road of balance is surely the best to choose, although the miser and the glutton never wish to find it: "So much for the man who would have none of God's help, but relied on his store of riches, and found his strength in knavery." [3]

Not only death is a bitter blow to the masterful art of survival, but suffering as well is a most dreaded guest at our dinner table. We just do not feel attracted to sit next to a cross, always afraid it may perturb too much the cozy symphony of health and vigor. Not even Christ was thrilled by the arrival of his disgraceful pains and deep afflictions: "And now he grew sorrowful and dismayed; my soul is ready to die with sorrow; do you abide here, and watch with me." [4] Perhaps Christ would have preferred at this precarious moment of redemption to save us without the sadness and the gloom which brought him so close to the abyss of annihilation: "Abba, Father, he said, all things are possible to thee; take away this chalice from before me; only as thy will is, not as mine is." [5]

Perhaps it was not only Christ who begged this heavenly Father to take away that bitter chalice, filled to the brim with agonies and death; we too, no doubt, have often burdened our lips with this eternal outcry of the hunted who has no corner left in which to hide. Take away this suffering we begged and cried, take

[3] Ps. 51. 9.
[4] Matt. 26. 38.
[5] Mark 14. 36.

it away from us as far as you can; we are too feeble to carry it further, we are too weak to bring it to the top of the bloody hill. Yes, we begged and begged, but the answer we received was silence. The wounds remained and the fire of our sorrows was not extinct. God did not deliver us from all the threats of darkness nor did he send an angel to soothe the bitter sting of pains and sorrows. Does God perhaps not hearken any more to our bursting cries of hunger and distress, or does he speak a tongue which we just fail to understand? Has he lost his interest the very moment a friend of his is facing the crucial test of his survival? Or is he intent to bring to our mind and heart a message we never wish to hear or learn?

There are two worlds which we know exist, the natural and the supernatural. There are two realms into which we are incorporated, the one we perceive and the other one which we do not see but which is yet so real. There are two kinds of attractive goods on our streets and markets, one we can buy and the other which is never sold away. There are two kinds of life, as there are two kinds of death, with neither ruling the other by sheer necessity, nor commanding by inevitable force. It is up to us to make the choice between the two, and our decision varies as much as the print of our fingers. Naturally, our number one concern is directed towards the world which surrounds us, which we can touch and enjoy, embrace in hours of enthusiasm and cast away in moments of disgust and failure. The realm of the visible possesses undeniably tremendous advantages over the "things invisible" and to no one's surprise are most of us in sympathy with our senses and wish them all the luck we can. The "natural" is just more appealing, much easier and warmer and it agrees so readily with everything we like to do. The "other world," so near and yet so far, which some refer to as illusion, is often exiled to the farthest sidelines of our life, and has to manage to survive there on a minimum of personal attention. No wonder that God is forced to readjustments. Since his concern is fixed around the world to come, he demonstrates much less anxiety about the world we see and love. Not that this natural life has evil roots, far be it so, but it is of less importance in the eternal scale of never-dying values. It is an echo rather than a voice, a shadow of a greater splendor.

If God prefers the supernatural, it is not just a luxury God can afford, but much more a logical appraisal of a prevailing situation. In the final collision, which is inevitable, the invisible world will triumph; the natural world, so dear to us now, will perish without a trace: "No, we do not play the coward; though the outward part of our nature is being worn down, our inner life is refreshed from day to day. This light and momentary affliction brings with it a reward multiplied every way, loading us with everlasting glory, if only we will fix our eyes on what is unseen, not on what we can see. What we can see lasts but for a moment; what is unseen is eternal." [6]

Perhaps we begin to grasp the meaning of the message of the heavenly Father? We even might commence to fathom the reason why He did not remove the chalice from our weary lips, although we begged him so dearly to do so. If this chalice, threatening as it may be, aids us in our supernatural conquest, why take it away? As a blessing in a wounded disguise, it can become the turning point of our whole destiny and even bring us to the point to which it brought the dying Christ when he prayed with total resignation: "Father into thy hands I commend my spirit."

Now is the propitious time to put our talents to the test and prove their worth in works of new creations.

Now is the acceptable time to employ our gifts to influence the lives of others and turn defeats to triumphs.

Now is the challenging hour in which all forces rally for survival.

But there comes a moment, perhaps not far away, in which activities and powers cease, and GOD alone will overpower all dimensions of existence with his tremendous love and mercy.

[6] 2 Cor. 4. 16–18.

FIFTEEN

How Great I Wish To Be

The population of heaven must be of great variety. With only one eternal city we are sure of, and with so manifold a diversity amongst us men, we are entitled to expect an exciting climate in the world to come. Perhaps we will meet there people whom God endowed with enormous riches but who were forever thoughtful and generous to the sorrows of the needy, while others, destitute themselves, could never alleviate the burdens of the hungry. Some, no doubt, robust and forceful in their zest for life, excelled in brilliant achievements of mortifications of which we only dare to think in our dreams; others, frail and tender in their strength, could never ponder over those exorbitant performances lest they endangered their own vitality and power. A great many, we may assume, secured their privilege to enter the heavenly city through their faithfulness in marriage; the remaining ones gained their admittance by strength of their virginity. Yet, as different as the picture may present itself, we are safe to presume that there is not one in heaven who was proud. Pride shuts the gates of the eternal paradise. As a leper is shunned by those who are not afflicted with this painful sickness and kept away from all the avenues of life, so is the proud one exiled from the roads of happiness and banished from the threshold of eternal bliss. Our Lord, aware of this tremendous danger, admonished us to learn from HIM, as he was "meek and humble of heart." In many situations he impressed on us, with his own determined action, how ugly and repulsive the mask of pride appears to him, and if we wish to learn this difficult and noble lesson we certainly find good material for our research. The one who argues that he never found a teacher is, no doubt, the greater fool.

All law aims at securing order. Pride alone is based on disorder. Firmly determined to gain something against the wish of the divine decree or to be something against the will of this supreme decision, it disregards completely eternal values and proportions. Pride steals. Thievery is the felony with which the defendant has to be prosecuted. The proud man not only deprives God of his rightful place in our heart but also takes from God an excellence which should never be divided into two: "Pride's beginning is man's revolt from God, when the heart forgets its Maker; and of all sin pride is the root." [1]

In pride we assert ourselves against the tremendous power which brought us into this existence and roughly brush aside the love which sustains us every minute of our precious being. "God made" is the label every human carries on his forehead and to our liking or dislike this label can never be removed again. To act as if WE had built our earthly dwelling is to inflate a zero to immense proportion and forget that it has only changed its size but not its inner value. Exaltation is often a dangerous adventure but it is most pitiful if it cuts the soul away from sources of real strength and power and decides to be self-sufficient from the outset to the end: "Thus there is no excuse for them; although they had the knowledge of God, they did not honour him or give thanks to him as God; they became fantastic in their notions, and their senseless hearts grew benighted; they who claimed to be so wise, turned fools." [2]

Pride is an innate propensity which is so often fatal since it penetrates and corrupts the whole character of a person. From its very roots man's heart is infected by a false degree of values, turning

[1] Ecclus. 10. 14.
[2] Rom. 1. 21–22.

the precious into the cheap and abandoning the highest for the lowest. Self-satisfaction has never ceased to be a hazard to men of all the centuries we count, and self-love was never outlawed from the boundaries of our nations. It is not difficult at all to perform acts of bravery and splendor if they enrich the glory of the name we carry, nor is it hard to accept applause for what we did to please our own requests and follies. To look down, without compassion, on those who are less fortunate and weak, is a temptation as old as age itself and rare they are who never indulged in this strange satisfaction. To be conceited of one's wisdom in a degree which never doubts that one is right is one of the prerogatives a proud mind takes for granted. Pride gives unfailing evidence of an extremely high degree of sensitivity, linked to a moodiness which is not only painful but dangerous as well. Proud people are so easily offended but hard to placate if their silly anger is aroused. With extravagant strength of temper they make life hard to bear for others and tensions follow swiftly where the proud has pitched his tent: "Poor fool, can axe set itself up against woodman, saw defy carpenter? Shall the rod turn on him who wields it, the staff, that is but wood, try conclusions with a living man." [3]

Pride is a perilous product to plant in our gardens. It spoils so much and yields so little. Useless on its own it becomes a serious threat to its surroundings as it renders ineffective everything it touches. The most fascinating performance inspired by conceit and pride is worthless in the sight of God. Why should God reward something which was not done for him? Why should he arrive as welcomed guest if no invitation was issued in his name? Why should he be pleased with a gift which we so gleefully present to ourselves? Every action, prompted by our own desire for glitter and for glory, carries neither power nor conviction and is at best an empty gesture pleasing only empty minds. Every deed based alone on talents we pretend to own is far below the reach of all the blessings from above, "Wilt thou toss thy head, bull-fashion, and glory in thy own strength? What if that strength should be brought down by thy own folly? Then wilt thou be no better than some dry tree-stump out in the desert, its leaves withered, its hope of fruits all gone." [4]

[3] Isa. 10. 15.
[4] Ecclus. 6. 2–3.

In a furious way our Lord lashed at the devil "pride," letting him know with no mistake, that he is a "trespasser" with no rights protecting his conceited path. Like a giant engaged in a fierce and embittered struggle, the ruler of heaven and earth accepts the irony of this uneven challenge and goes through all the strategy of a triumphant conqueror who never lost a battle, "Dwelling where thou dost in the clefts of the rocks, thou art puffed up with pride; high thou has built thy throne and thinkest there is none can drag thee down to earth. Build thy eyrie high as the eagle, nest, if thou wilt, amongst the stars, I will yet drag thee down thence, the Lord says." [5]

The proud one does not fully realize the "odds" against his desperate adventure; otherwise he never dared to write the name of God amongst his bitter enemies. Blinded by the sun of his own making, he lost the rays of the eternal light, and knowing only shadows, he misses nothing but himself. Withdrawing from the magnet of real life and power, he flees into the centers of his own, hoping to find there another captain who can save the threatened bark of life. Sure of himself beyond advice, he never begs for help or counsel, and in rare moments only is he aware that he has made himself the victim of his own deception. Gradually it dawns on him how little influence and power he really wields on others, and all too soon he shows that he is governed and sustained by the compulsive need of his own craving passions. A benevolent king, willing to rule with mercy and compassion, was banished so that a stubborn tyrant could dictate with malice and confusion: "Now indeed man's haughty looks must fall to earth, human pride must be abated, no room for any greatness but the Lord's, when that day comes. The day of the Lord of hosts! With the dawn of it all human pomp and state must be overshadowed, all human magnificence grow dim." [6]

In order to castigate the man of pride, God needs no swords or fighting angels; it is entirely sufficient to leave the proud man to himself. Alone he can do nothing. Abandonment by God is one of the more cruel things a proud one has to face, and it is fatal to the man who reconciles his soul to its results. To spell forever only his own name and see no more but his own face in all the mirrors

[5] Abdias 1. 3–4.
[6] Isa. 2. 11–12.

on the walls, to hear but one echo from all the mountains of the world, this is the terrible price one has to pay for this cursed punishment of heaven. To be deserted by a friend, especially in need and danger, creates some hardships, as we know, but to be forsaken by the mighty God himself, this is so terrible a thought that we beg and pray we never have to entertain it. Man's greatest felicity consists in the conversion of his restless mind to God and the greatest tragedy in his life occurs when this same mind turns defiantly against its maker. What can man still think about if he is not able anymore to think of God and heaven? How desolate the world must look to pride which gazes at this brilliant display of sparkling beauties with eyes closed by its own blindness. To say to darkness "Be my light" and curse the light as darkness, this is the climax pride can ever reach and there seem to be enough in our midst who are its ready victims. Their sense of danger must be dormant, or they would never greet their ugly death as resurrection. Even Christ admitted willingly that all those human sinners who nailed him to the cross in order to mock and blaspheme him there, "did not know what they were doing" as their wisdom was their ignorance. Lack of knowledge may in the end be the only advocate who can plead to God for mercy: "I was wretched and every soul is wretched that is bound in affection of mortal things: it is tormented to lose them and in their loss becomes aware of the wretchedness which in reality it had even before it lost them. And I wept most bitterly and in that bitterness found my only repose."[7] Our modern agnostics who do not weep, but despair, can learn at least from St. Augustine if they refuse to learn from Christ.

God wants forever our emptiness and never seeks the plenitude which we imagine we possess. He begs for our hunger and yearns for our thirst but has no use for our vain abundance. To know about what we really are and to understand to express it clearly is a wisdom rarely found in our midst. A child was once declared as heaven's ideal, not on account of years but for sincerity and innocence. He can not hide or twist his soul but shows so freely what he thinks or loves. We, whose years have accumulated, are often judged MATURE if we acquired the technic to hide. Not to

[7] Conf. 4. 6.

126

present what really is behind our name but painting wishful dreams, exalting our own position and resenting anything which lowers it, this is the ideal we have fabricated and to this man-made image we clutch as drowning men clutch at a straw. Castles in the air and fairy tales are welcome guests in our spiced narrations, but mistakes we made are swiftly justified in our own imagination and blamed on those who did not know enough. We lead our own life for our own purpose and forget so readily that God has said: "I am the Lord, whose name tells of power; I will not let the boast that is mine pass to another, or share my renown with graven gods." [8]

If pride is really such a ruthless enemy of man, how can we liberate our hearts from its destructive claws and free our mind from its relentless threats and dangers? Is it really possible to defy its potent might and become the man God wishes me to be? Can I ever translate my whole being into this precious virtue of humility and act in full dependence on God's omnipotent authority? With the graces of God I certainly can, but without them I will never gain the necessary insight into my own condition nor will I ever learn the deeper meaning of my proper name. I have to pray to become humble, pray as hard and as intensely as I have never prayed before in my whole existence. In the end, which arrives so soon, it may be these humble prayers which will safeguard my eternal joy in heaven. If it is true that God holds the arrogant man in constant abomination, it is equally true that he likes and loves the humble: "My son, do all thou dost in lowly fashion. The greater thou art, the more in all things abase thyself; so thou shalt win favour with God. Sovereignty belongs to God and no other; they honor him most that most keep humility." [9]

To assert that prayers open the golden road of humility and combat the vice of pride most effectively does not exclude our willingness to accept humiliations if they are on the way to our doors. In order to develop and to deepen this greatest of all virtues we have to be eager and alert to practice it, not only in our thoughts but in our deeds as well. We know only too well that our lips, even when dressed in pious moods, can easily mislead our judgment and a most touching parade of words can readily hide an ugly mask. Fox

[8] Isa. 42. 8.
[9] Ecclus. 3. 19–21.

and lamb have all too often exchanged their customs and we have hardly known the difference. Our readiness to accept humiliations graciously and our eagerness to fulfill our duties faithfully, even in adverse conditions, would indicate that our inner values and desires are genuine and strong. Moreover, if we are slow to disguise our limitations and not hesitant at all to admit them freely to all others, we reveal a sincerity and calm which even could disarm the fearful might of God: "Honour is for those that honour me, for those that make light of me, only contempt." [10] The great ones however in our midst, we might call them saints, not only accept humiliations patiently, but also go out of their way to seek their presence eagerly and invite them to their table as we invite beloved guests. Convinced of the significance of this eternal treasure, they would give themselves up completely to gain possession of this coveted virtue. The proud of mind would invent their pride if it did not yet exist. To bow to God is the one concession pride is never in the mood to make. In hasty ignorance, humility is marked as weakness, forgetting willingly that this very weakness is a sign of strength: "But if anyone, citizen or alien, is guilty of an offence through pride, and in a spirit of rebellion against the Lord, he is lost to his people. Would he despise the Lord's word, annul his commandment? That fault deserves death, and he will be held to account for it." [11]

Great caution is advised, however, before we finally declare a man's behavior as proud. Just as exterior exhibit of humility not always indicates the virtue, so does not every indication of arrogance and pride pass as a vice or mortal sin. It happens more than we think that man's uncertainty of mind and heart is often camouflaged as haughtiness and exaltation, while youthful quest for admiration defends itself behind disdain and self-elation. Conditioned by a lack of years, the younger ones drive hard to impress all others with the little they possess and, sensing their inferiority, call on complacency to fill the blatant vacancy. This self-deception is, no doubt a sign of immaturity but in its roots it is as harmless as their boyish boasting. Great understanding paired with a sense of real compassion is more advisable than dire

[10] I Kings 2. 30.
[11] Num. 15. 30–31.

threats with weary admonitions. The more reserved we appear in our judgment, the more influential we seem to be. Perhaps we even discover behind the outer rind of bold defiance a surprising depth of docility and submission. The selfless man will easily know the difference and he will be the best help to guide the youthful fire.

Man is the being who carries in his heart a world far greater than he knows. What he reveals through all his open deeds and secret actions is only part of all the treasures entrusted to his vigilance and care. We contemplate so often nothing but the fruits a tree has borne. Our Lord looks at the roots from which the tree has sprung. No wonder that divine reactions have often differed deeply from all the calculations of the world. How well fared sinful Magdalene compared with the austere, religious Pharisee who led a life of discipline and order. How quickly was a thief rushed into heaven, while many noble souls were waiting centuries to enter their celestial reward. Not that we presume to read the mind of God in these decisions, but do we not come close to a true answer if we distinguish sins of weakness from sins committed by one's strength.

In sins of strength the power of the mind is at the root of our judgment and the decisions which are made are based on long reflections of the reason. Enough time is granted to the intellect to get acquainted with the situation and take a stand in favor of the issue or against it. Excusing elements are absent from the threshold of one's judgment and behind the final verdict stands every letter of the name who signed. The Pharisee, refusing Christ, was not excused by ignorance but had to take the full responsibility for his defiant stand against the life of the Redeemer. Like many an agnostic, he knew what he was doing and he did it. With all the power of his will and knowledge he prosecuted Christ and signed the warrant of his death like any other document, which helped his pride to survive: "Woe upon you, you Pharisees, for loving the first seats in the synagogues, and to have your hands kissed in the market-place; woe upon you, that are like hidden tombs which men walk over without knowing it." [12]

The sin of weakness is of other structure. Not only is the mind the culprit on the scene but our senses too are deeply involved

[12] Luke 11. 43–44.

in our ultimate decision. Our Lord, so human in so many realms of life, was well aware of our nature's strength and frailty and rarely showed his surprise when it turned violent or ugly. He knew so well how swiftly our agitated senses correspond to lures and irritations and how little time is granted to the reason to exert its influence and might. It is not rare that the tremendous strength of intellect is dimmed by all the fog of lust and fascination and drawn into decisions which later on are followed by regrets and tears. Have we not often heard one to confess in bitter disgust with oneself "Why did I do that" or "How could I have done it"? Is not the storeroom of our memories filled to the brim with deeds we like so little since they remind us so much of our foolish plays with unruly instincts and hungry passions? Was it the Lord alone who was offended by the misdeeds of my stubborn senses or did I hurt my own ideal, so strong in dreams and feeble yet when pressured by my passions and illicit joys: "Because of all this my soul was sick, and broke out in sores, whose itch I agonized to scratch with the rub of carnal things — carnal, yet if there were no soul in them, they would not be objects of love." [13]

Once, sin of strength met sin of weakness in a room as wide as all the walls of our world. A Pharisee, pleased with his superiority, rebuked our Lord for letting a sinful woman touch his skin: "If this man were a prophet he would know who this woman is that is touching him, and what kind of woman, a sinner." Our Lord being a prophet and even more than a prophet knew well enough who knelt so humbly at his feet as he was also fully conscious of the mentality of the "perfect man," who was so deeply pained by the presence of this sinful creature. Frail this woman was, no doubt, but she knew it; the Pharisee felt so strong that he forgot his weakness. Who was in greater danger? Who was more exposed to imminent perdition, humble knowledge or affected ignorance? Who will receive merciful forgiveness, the one who admitted or the other who accused? Our Lord, registering first a few complaints against omitted rituals of welcome, looked at the Pharisee and said, "If great sins have been forgiven her, she has also greatly loved. He loves little, who has little forgiven him. Then he said to her, Thy sins are forgiven." [14]

[13] Conf. 3. 1.
[14] Luke 7. 39–47.

How differently these two varied people must have set out on their way home on this great day when they met their Lord and Master; one with a lesson learned, the other with a lesson wasted. Who of these resembles me the most? Who of these resembles you?

Humility and pride are two vast movements of the human mind which deeply influence the course of human history. Strong like the wings of hurricanes and swift as soaring missiles, they aim at heights so dazzling and sublime that not even angels resist their alluring fascination. Inconspicuous in their beginning, they readily establish their colossal power and, sooner than we think, exert their influence on every page of time. Relentless in their fiery passions, they never lay their head to rest unless all others have been drawn into the orbit of their world-wide vision. Triumphs, no doubt, they have achieved, but never has humility penetrated heaven so deeply as at this mighty moment when God himself bowed to its majestic invitation: "Be it done unto me according to thy wish." Humility invited Christ to live. Pride condemned Christ to an early death. So fearful are the powers of the two.

Great WE will be if we dare to be little; small we remain if we pretend to be great.

May God, in wisdom and in mercy, impart to us the grace to make the choice which is not only best for us but for all others too, who are a part of our eternal destiny.

SIXTEEN

The Attic And
The Old Blind Woman

In a poor and shabby looking attic, high above the noisy street
dwelt a little old woman who was blind. A creaky table in the
dusty corner and an outworn chair next to the heavy wooden
door only deepened the gloom which kept the walls so bleak and
lowered so deeply the ceiling. Even the speedy rays of the golden
sun suffered many a frustrated moment until they could find the
little panes of the beaten windows and managed to rest in this
shabby attic and warm the wrinkles of the little old lady.

As sad as this attic looked, it never affected the inner world
of this woman at all. Sorrow and grief were never invited to share
the path of her lonely and forgotten life. It was spring, eternal
spring, which kept her heart in bloom and painted her cheeks so
surprisingly rosy. Asked once by a friend, "What has God given
to you today?" She answered with a smile, "A plate full of onion
soup which was a trifle too cold, a large slice of bread and a faith
as deep as a lake." Pressed a little harder about the number of
complaints hidden away in her good heart but ready to be revealed at her judgment day, she swiftly replied, "I have no com-

plaints." "What about your eyes which are dead while there is still so much life beating in your pulse? Do you not realize what you miss? You are not allowed to cherish the splendid harmony of colors which graces so much the pretty cheeks of our flowers nor can you drink of the majestic innocence of our fiery glaciers nor is it granted to you to gauge the depths of the horizons or twinkle at the pillows of the never resting clouds. All the grandeur has escaped your eyes and you will miss it forever."

"I miss nothing," was the swift reply of the blind woman and after a pause which was not long and yet so heavy, she repeated firmly, "I miss nothing. I have experienced so much in my lonely years; thus I have so much to read. The pages of my life are in a dark binding and so many a chapter is marked with a cross, but my last page, I hope, will carry a beautiful crown."

This sounded like her testament. Neither jewels nor money could she bequeath to others, as she was so poor herself, but faith, deep, blind faith, was the treasure she was so eager and willing to share. It was true, she could not read the books of learned men, but she could read so well the lessons which our Lord himself wrote in her humble heart.

Impressed by the golden wisdom of this little old woman who could not see, we begin to peruse the pages we have written during the storms and triumphs of our life. Carefully our eyes search through the chapters we composed and scrutinize events which long ago have happened and which will never be forgotten. Sentence after sentence is critically screened and word after word is discreetly pondered. Alert, as never before, we recognize that we are the authors of this book and that we alone are responsible for the content of this volume. No one else is allowed to substitute for our name.

"The pages of my life are in a dark binding" we hear the woman in the attic say, and without much reflection or concern, we realize that our book of life is shaded with the same obscurity, Night fell upon us so often although the sun was shining.

Darkness stands for mystery, and a journey through darkness is a journey through fear. We are afraid of enemies who hide behind the wings of night, as we are afraid of ourselves when dawn is our only cover. Days without the rays of the sun or nights without the beams of the moon are thorny to explore and difficult to seize. Who has not sensed the fearful loneliness which overcomes our soul when darkness creeps along the walls of our empty room and makes us shiver under its heavy load of broken dreams and failures. Who was never tempted to curse with his strangled breath the misery of his own destiny? Was it not night when Judas betrayed his Lord! Was it not darkness which covered our betrayals and our sins?

In its gentler mood, however, darkness presents a lenient face of relief. It appeases the mind which has lost its bearing and brings the sleep of rest to eyes of guilt and shame. Have we not often concealed the unrest of our biting conscience behind the strange security of a stormy night? Have we not greedily accepted the empty protection which dark clouds, on a listless sky, offered to our shameful hours. Whatever mission darkness has performed in our life, hostile or friendly, it surely did not belong to the nobler hours of our existence, as it was only a last escape for a man who lost his way. The coward in us was calling for its fateful presence and the same coward enjoyed its blind protection: "How they shun the light, these rebels who ignore God's precepts, leave his path untrodden! The murderer must be stirring before daybreak, to catch his helpless prey, or prowl, as the thieves prowl, at night. For darkness, too, the adulterer waits, no eye must scan his muffled features; under cover of darkness he will break into the house, to keep the tryst made yesterday; no daylight for him. To him the first flush of dawn is death's shadow; deep gloom is the sunshine he walks by." [1] Not all the sharing of darkness in our life was created by our own folly. Many a riddle was written without our pen, and various perplexing questions were asked without our lips.

Nature, secure in its own laws and regulations and charmed with its tremendous beauties, unfolds to us so many puzzling questions that we fall forever short in our efforts to secure solutions. As two thousand years ago, the wise men of today are still trying to decode the glittering language of our golden stars, and many a genius capitulated in front of the majestic secrets which

[1] Job 24. 13–17.

our brilliant universe projected into the midst of our mysterious orbit. The ever-changing face of our seasons, which thrill the gifted mind of our poets and spell disasters with their storms and furies, is still an enigma to so many who wish to read and predict the path of behaviour. The rumbling of the volcanoes, which in their eruptive wrath have harried once a civilization and still bring death to all who walk their glowing stream, is shrouded with the clouds of mysteries which we are just beginning to decipher. Let us not forget the pretty little flower whose tender face was burned so badly and we, not knowing how to restore its beauty, let sadly wither away. It is true that the genius of our civilization has lifted many veils from the mysteries of nature, only to find out that after one successful discovery, another secret challenges the depth and daring of the human mind. The more we read, the more we realize that there are many pages left which we are not yet able to discern.

People can offer darkness either as their gift of passion or as the token of their greed. A trusted friend suddenly forgets his promise and lets his smile freeze to a threat. The warmth and kindness of a neighbor's goodness disappears swiftly, to be replaced by coldness and indifference. My only brother, whose precious love has brightened so many days of my past, changes his heart, and while changing, breaks my own. Have not all of us experienced, at least once in our life, the fickleness of human feelings and emotions? Were we never fooled by the restless beat of the human heart? Why did we admit on this unlucky day of our career that we lost a friend? And with the friend, a world has perished.

Equally confusing is, at times, the look of enemies. More than once has a defiant heart turned into an open welcome, and more than once has bitter hatred mellowed into tender love. Where we expected a bristling NO as the reply, we were offered a gentle YES, and when we were firmly set for a long and dreary winter, we discovered the promising signs of a lovely spring. Perhaps it would be wise never to declare a man an enemy forever. Have we not seen, again and again, how freely hostile camps of war change into partners of the future. Are not our recent happenings in history a proof of the uncertainty of friend and enemy?

Strangest of all, however, is the man in the street in my life, who brings neither light nor darkness. He is so near to me that I can never miss him, and yet he is so far away that I am never able to find his soul. I know his name and like his manners. I recognize his house and pass his street four times a day. I am impressed with many features of his skill and I express my admiration for his talents. We shake each other's hand and share our hearty laughter, only to realize at the end of our meetings that we are strangers to each other, strangers, who never did exchange hearts. No challenge is offered from the shores of our life and the sun is not able to shine in its power; only grayish clouds are drifting along in a pallid sky.

One riddle still remains on the horizon of my weary mind, a riddle which is not concerned with man or nature. Great and wide as the heaven above, it surely is the hardest to solve and the most arduous to comprehend. It is God Himself. How will he judge me if he sees me as I really am, without my mask and without all my pretentious speech? What does he think of me at this very moment, and what is my idea about him right now? Is not all my knowledge about the Divine, even after years of studies, incomplete and poor? Who can ever say that he has comprehended, at last, the incomprehensible? Never to be sure, and yet to hope forever, this seems to be the only thing which is really certain in my fate. God stands often before me like a huge, dark forest, difficult to discover, and hard to penetrate, or he appears to me like a majestic peak of a great mountain-range, imposing and superb, but inaccessible and profoundly silent. No doubt, this my Lord and Master is a great blessing, with his benign and humble love, but he can also be my threat and danger if he insists on meeting me on that stormy hill which is crowned with a bloody cross, the sign of his redemption: "Lord I lie open to thy scrutiny; thou knowest me, knowest when I sit down and when I rise up again, canst read my thoughts from far away. If I could wing my way eastwards or find a dwelling beyond the western sea, still would I find thee beckoning to me, thy right hand upholding me. Or perhaps I would think to bury myself in darkness; night should surround me, friendlier than day; but no, darkness is no hiding-place from thee, with thee the night shines clear as day itself; light and dark are one." [2]

[2] Ps. 138. 2 and 9–12.

136

Looking back again into the dim attic of the woman who was blind, we hear her say in her resigned, old voice: "Many a chapter in the book of my life is marked with the sign of a cross."

Like monuments in history, the cross marks our way of life. No one's existence is entirely free of tears. Have not all of us accumulated times of sufferings, over which we cried so loudly or cursed so bitterly? We weep perhaps in stern defiance of our fate and destiny, whereas some others shed their tears in hunger and in pain. Few there are who cry while they are silly, and many weep for reasons which are small and simple. Yet tears remain tears and they are bitter to everyone, as no one likes to be in pain or hurt by trials and afflictions.

Crosses are as different as the minds of the people who carry them. If some have speculated wrongly on the market of quick fortunes and lost much more than they are able to afford, they readily complain about a cross they have to carry, instead of admitting that they have made a costly error, for which they have to pay a heavy price. Others again are agitated and perturbed in their peace of mind by bitter memories of smart decisions, which aided them so much to be successful in their world of dreams but hurt the chances of the next one who had to starve in want and in despair. Duties return to our mind and haunt us like a ghost, because we bypassed them so cleverly and let some others pay our debts. Or we were fleeing from the heat of battle since we were hopeless cowards, and now we are not able to forget the face of the man who died while he defended the abandoned post. Pains might begin to knock at our heart to indicate that enemies have penetrated our vital stream of blood to lay waste the health of our body, and we are helpless victims of a cross which stands as sign of triumph on the hill of Calvary: "All about me surged the waves of death, deep flowed the perilous tide, to daunt me; the grave had caught me in its toils, deadly snares had trapped my feet. One cry to the Lord, in my affliction, one word of summons to my God, and he, from his sanctuary, listened to my voice; the complaint I made before him found a hearing." [3]

Some chapters in our book of life begin with crosses which we ourselves have laid on our own shoulders, without the wish of our Lord. Someone needed us and begged for our help and we

[3] Ps. 17. 5–7.

possessed enough to give, but we preferred to shut the windows of our soul and stay hardened to the cries of misery and hunger. A wounded friend perhaps expected us much more than our gift of flowers, and while he waited eagerly for our consolations, we wasted our time with cheap banalities and foolish trifles. Our enemies might have been willing and prepared to sign a pact of peace and bury the war of the past, whereas we, with our sense of pride and feelings of revenge, made the approach of better times a failure. Perhaps the heaviest cross of our modern world is waiting for our shoulders, the cross which does not adorn a hill, but rises up from the very center of our hearts . . . the cross of not loving any more. For this detestable sin of not loving, of not caring for the needs of others, there is no punishment on earth, because the law we break was made in a world far greater than the world we live in. It must be terrible to hear from God the fateful sentence: "Thou art cursed because you never gave your heart to others." Not to live is bad enough, but not to love is worse.

As a grateful gesture of farewell, we approached once more the blind, old woman in the attic and asked her gently to repeat the final sentence she spoke. With a smile which was so far beyond her poverty and solitude, she said, almost in a whisper: "My last page, I hope, will carry a graceful crown."

Life can be so beautiful because it can end so well. Even if our days are accompanied by heavy threats of tempests and defeats, we should never feel disheartened as we are always going TO THE LIGHT. Our wandering through the night is never endless, but terminated by the rays of hope, announcing jubilantly the arrival of a better day. The deeper meaning of our existence is success and not defeat. For triumphs we are born and not for destruction. Life is not a regrettable waste of boring hours and of senseless days, worthy only to be thrown away like the peel of a fruit or the wrappings of a box. Life is much more than the thrill of the moment in which we forget so quickly the nobility of our character, and remember so promptly the instincts of the beast. Life on earth is only the beginning of a felicity and joy which is so beautiful that it must endure forever.

The atheist resigns himself to end his days in a big and muddy hole, deep enough to bury his tottering bones and wide enough to cover up his bloodless nerves. Concerned only about the hunger in the streets of this world, he never strained his eyes to gaze at the world beyond. The charming paradise on earth, where everyone receives what he desires, is the only dream he cherishes, and in this self-made dream, nothing is of greater value than his own selfish hunger. The hated end of an aimless life is perhaps tragic for the wishful atheist, but he accepts this dreary fact as inevitable and final. Like the last stroke of a bell, the heart of man gives its last beat, and then the exciting gamble is over and perhaps lost. For the child of God, however, the end of life means only a beginning, a fresh start for the life everlasting. "Vita non tollitur sed mutatur — life is not taken away from us but changed." Changed into the eternal bliss of heaven where we will see God face to face. This view of God in his fascinating splendor and omnipotence may well be the very climax of my whole existence. In comparison with this greatest moment of my life, nothing else on earth really matters. All my cares and trials in this valley of tears are only part of my final preparation, in which God tests the strength of my heart and examines the secret thoughts of my never-resting mind. In a little while, as our Lord stated, this trial will be over, and then, after all the storms have passed, I will gather my bounteous harvest and accept my beautiful reward — the crown of eternal joy in heaven. "Then I saw a new heaven and a new earth. The old heaven, the old earth had vanished and there was no more sea. And I, John, saw in my vision that holy city which is the new Jerusalem, being sent down by God from Heaven, all clothed in readiness, like a bride who has adorned herself to meet her husband. I heard, too, a voice which cried aloud from the throne, here is God's tabernacle pitched among men; he will dwell with them, and they will be his own people, and he will be among them, their own God. He will wipe away every tear from their eyes and there will be no more death, or mourning or cries of distress, no more sorrow; those old things have passed away." [4]

[4] Apoc. 21. 1–5.

SEVENTEEN

Are My Words A Prayer

The might of a nation is so often proportioned to the might of the hands which are folded. The Romans were at the pinnacle of their glorious power when prayer held an honored position in the disciplined heart of their illustrious empire, and their steps were powerful and mighty as long as their iron legions kept prayers in deepest esteem and in highest glory. Only when the temples were allowed to fall into ruins, and when prayers were not heard any more in their public domain, a decline in politics and morals set in, which in the end crushed the magnificent empire into a gigantic heap of ruins.

Nations are only the harvest of families. Dissipate the energy of this consecrated union and you fritter away the vigor and the spirit of the most powerful lands. The edge of a sword alone can never provide eternal security; it will aways need the indomitable force of our hallowed families, which keep secure the peace on our troubled borders. Will the womb of a blessed family ever produce a brood of ugly traitors?

What keeps a family so strong and mighty? What inspires them to remain together faithfully until death releases their hearts from their solemn vows? No other power than the unbreakable force of their common prayers. The hands that beg God together are strong and kind enough to beg for each other. Prayer is the holy meeting place for those who need one another, and it is the point of fulfillment for those who love each other. There is a reverence about this holy and mysterious union with God which reflects itself so deeply in the reverence which children show to their parents and parents show to each other. One given to prayer will not be arrogant or domineering, but humble and sincerely modest, since in his discourse with the Divine he learns the gentle art of serving.

Prayer aims at a mysterious world, so near to our heart, and yet so far from our reach. We are not allowed to enter and to penetrate those secret boundaries, since our soul is still contained in its precarious vessel of clay. Our thoughts, however, and our wishes, our triumphs and our defeats, our love and our hatred, can be translated into the golden key which opens so gently the secret gates of heaven, and penetrates those endless depths beyond which we can not see, but only hope and believe. Prayer is really a magnificent discovery of a land which has yet to come into existence in our life. It is a safe and hallowed return to the cradle which gave us the hour of our beginning. In a certain sense prayer brings the future into our presence, and, to no one's surprise, some great souls have returned from their hour of discourse with God with the story of their future on their chastened lips.

Prayer is the most challenging activity of the human mind. To search for the secrets of God is a far greater command than to search for the secrets of our planets. In our halls of science and in our shiny laboratories we only trace the wondrous imprints of our Lord on the face of our orbit; in prayer and meditation we try to read the mind of God himself. The brilliant gift of intellect, which exalts man so highly above the brute, was bestowed upon us in order to discover and to know. Restless like the majestic waves of the turbulent sea, the mind of man pitches furiously against the edge of the unknown and ebbs away to peace after the answers are wrestled from the mysterious depths and the veil of secret is lifted. But can God ever be exhausted? Can his terrifying might ever be brought into an all-embracing formula which finally explains all the mysterious garments of the heavens above?

141

Can we ever hope to find the magic number which tames the power of the King of Kings? Once, a day might rise when the genius in man can triumphantly proclaim that the puzzles of the universe are solved and that all the question marks in our books are ultimately erased, but the bells will never ring the hour when men can rejoice in the thought of having completely fathomed God. Even after our most intense investigation, after all the reading of the books, our thoughts about God remain the thoughts of little children. "How deep is the mine of God's wisdom, of his knowledge; how inscrutable are his judgments, how undiscoverable his ways! Who has ever understood the Lord's thoughts or been his counsellor?" [1]

As long as heaven issues this unconquerable challenge, the mind of man will never cease to pray. Awed by the regal grandeur of God's majesty, and deeply inspired by the power of his love, man the crown of his creation will always feel the need to worship and to adore. Christians and pagans might share nothing else with each other but the burning thirst for the mysteries of the Divine. In the hearts of both, the desire to know more about God is the greatest desire of all. "To thee I appealed, and thou didst listen to me, didst fill my heart with courage. All the kings of the earth, Lord, will praise thee now; were not thy promises made in their hearing?" [2]

In prayer we feel secure. A portion of heavenly peace and tranquility descends into our own frail and precarious existence, conveying to our mind such confidence and serenity that the storms of life do not disturb us any more. Not that we become indifferent or numb to the needle of life — this would be a lamentable victory — but we learn, under the blessed roof of heaven, how to accept and how to endure the decision of the divine will which is so often very different from our own inclinations and desires. To submit ourselves to this "greater will than ours" is the characteristic of the strong and holy. Only a man without fear can say to God, "Speak oh Lord, thy servant listens."

The man who never prays is either ignorant or conceited. If foolishness perturbs his mind, he carries no responsibility but if

[1] Rom. 11. 33–34.
[2] Ps. 137. 3–4.

pride hardens his lips, he is cursed. The proud man who boasts to own so many talents and feels so rich and safe in his possessions is not intent to leave an inch to God and His divine designs. The harvest of his fields provides his abundant sustenance, and hunger has no permit to step beyond his fences. His blessings are his own; let God's concern be with the poor and wretched. Why be a humble beggar and pray if one can be so strong a master and command? "My God, break their cruel fangs; Lord shatter their jaw, strong as the jaw of lions. Like spilt water, let them run to waste." [3]

Some shun away from God and never want to hear his name again because they have abandoned their own fate first and care no more for what will happen afterwards. Like rats on a sinking ship, they hasten away from their drowning conscience and seek their solace in their flesh and its desires. Their weakness is not always malice, but grim despair looks through their weary eyes. They gamble and they gamble with those sticky cards which spell the name — "inferno."

Not to pray is pitiable, but to pray with a false heart is worse. The weakling, who hides from God because he is afraid and ashamed to pray, can often be closer to God than the man who prays but does not mean it. To be a liar is ugly enough, but to make God a partner of my lie, is detestable. To approach the majestic grounds of the holy tabernacle with a mask on our face is so grotesque that it should only happen on a stage or in a circus. If we continue, however, to deceive God with a false image, we should not be surprised if we hear from our Lord the fateful sentence — "I know you not." How can God know us if we are not ourselves? How can he recognize us if we are so strange to our own mind and heart? Some have twisted their souls so much that their lips do not know any more what they say or what they promise. "They honor me with their lips but their hearts are afar from me."

Prayer loves solitude and silence. The precious discourse with God has not the sound of heavy-footed steps on a noisy flight of bulky stairs, but is a rather quiet turning of our lips and our mind to God. A rumbling flood of words will only tire our tongues and

[3] Ps. 57. 8.

never touch or influence the hallowed mind of God. If we speak much, we think little. Not that the spoken word is to be shunned as superfluous or dangerous. To pray is to communicate with God and our power of communication is the verbal expression. But, with the word, our thoughts must fly to heaven; otherwise, we babble like the Gentiles who want to be heard by God on account of their wordiness. Our Lord warned us explicitly not to become like them. The prayer which erupts from the depths of our heart, unrehearsed and spontaneous, is perhaps the best of all the gifts we have to offer, and such a prayer will always find its own appropriate expression. There are, however, hours when our minds are arid and fatigued and we feel weary and exhausted, with our hearts as empty as a shell. In such moments of distress and dire need, when not even short ejaculations arise from our burdened minds, we should accept the gentle help from sources which others have laid open for our own discretion, and which our holy Mother the Church has wisely approved and blessed. The prayers of others, printed in stately books or revealed in beautiful hymns, can lead our searching minds into a blissful discovery of wonders which God has worked so triumphantly in the hearts of others. Whatever the source of our inspiration, whether we read from our hearts or pray from pages of a book, we should always address God as a friend who understands our hunger and knows of our thirst. If we are not allowed to pour forth our daily needs and trials into the merciful abyss of God's love and understanding, where else can we go to find an echo of our cries? "Where shall we go Master, you have words of eternal life."

Our actions have to proceed from a source. Somewhere they have to be grounded. The man who prays discovers in his heart a wonderful measure for eternity. Firmly rooted in the secure balance of the supernatural world, he is calm when he is confronted with the ever-pressing call for action! The hours, disappearing by the ticking clock, lose their hasty steps and become precious friends, teaching him the value of eternity and alerting him to the fleeting glitter of the days and years. Even the man of brilliant action has to seek the might of the winter when nature, covered with the gentle white, restores so quietly the waning vigor of her tired pulse. Haste alone, without a seed, is sterile. Useful perhaps to nimble fingers, and exciting to loud and vulgar lips, it does not possess the power to create the immortal achievements which grace so much the illustrious efforts of the human genius. In the superficial era we are living in, we try to speed up every beat of our heart, but we will forever fail if we attempt to speed up greatness. God who is eternal has time and takes it, whereas, we, lost in our little inches, are forever hunted by our rush and hurry. "Once when he had found a place to pray in, one of his disciples said to him, after his prayer was over, Lord, teach us how to pray." [4] Joining this disciple we beg from God the same instruction, and with our ready heart accept the lessons which we learn from the greatest Master.

We are before man what we are before the eyes of God. The man who knows how to pray well will serve man with honor and nobility. If we keep faithfully our promises to God, we will not abandon the friend whom God has entrusted to our hearts. Can we ever trust a man who hates to speak to his Lord and Master? What can he offer to us if he has nothing to offer to God? High sounding phrases perhaps, put into the catchy rhythm of a song, or vain dreams of an earthly paradise, where everyone takes as much as he is able, till nothing else is left but hatred. Can the man who has shut the gate of heaven present anything but the narrowness of his own name, which is so dismally smaller than the majestic name of God?

Prayers can never be measured or stopped by the pointers of a clock. This most beautiful activity of man is not under the law of our minutes and hours but under the wings of human freedom. If we pray, we are above time, and hours can easily turn into seconds, if God in his kindness and mercy graces the soul with his benevolent presence. Yet there are particular moments in the course of a day which God especially desires for an appointment with us — sunrise and sunset. The morning, which presents to us the spring of life, should commence with the blessings from above, while the evening, which brings us to the thought of death, should close its tired eyes with a hymn of thanks. If God is faithfully invited to close the hours of my days, he will not be too far away if I beg him to seal the story of my life. If my last words on earth

[4] Luke 11. 1.

are prayers, what can I lose? And Simeon said, blessing God: "Ruler of all, now dost thou let thy servant go in peace, according to thy word; for my eyes have seen that saving power of thine which thou hast prepared in the sight of all nations. This is the light which shall give revelation to the gentiles, this is the glory of thy people Israel." [5]

Prayer is not an old and venerable tale of charming fairies and busy angels, nor is it a cleverly calculated means to keep the poor and hungry begging for the bread of heaven, and induce them to forget their share of the crust of the earth. Prayer is as real as God is. Only if we call God a liar will our prayers be a lie. If our belief in the might of God is firmly rooted in depths of our soul, we will never doubt, nor hesitate to approach the Lord in the hour of our need, and beg him for his help and his assistance. Quickly we return with thankful hearts if triumphs strike our fate and if success remains with our uncertain future. "Ask and the gift will come; seek and you shall find; knock and the door shall be opened to you. Everyone that asks, will receive; that seeks, will find; that knocks will have the door opened to him." [6] If, at certain moments of our life, we despair in God because he does not seem to answer our prayers let us never forget that — NO — was his answer. Why should God never be allowed to say "NO" to my requests?

Our powerful nation is able to afford a style of living which is perhaps the most envied one in this struggling universe. Surrounded by an affluence which alleviates human hardships to an astonishing degree, we enjoy an ease in living which is excellent and dangerous at the same time. By our very instincts we can so readily become the helpless victims of our ever-growing appetites and lose the discipline we need to master our restless hunger. Impressed like children by the material size of our magnificent achievements, we are prone to forget that real greatness can never be expressed in size and numbers only. May the generation which follows our path never accuse us of having instructed them well in all the arts of human wisdom but we forgot to teach them the greatest art of all — how to pray.

[5] Luke 2. 29–32.
[6] Matt. 7. 7–8.

EIGHTEEN

The Year When It is Young

In our life, time is a guest who is always present although it never is invited to arrive. Once with us it stays and never takes a leave of absence nor has it ever need of rest or a vacation. To delegate its precious powers into the hands of other rulers is a thought it never entertained in its career on earth. Time has no name and yet embraces all the names. It has no size and still embraces all the mountains and the shores of all the seas. Full of charm and beauty it fascinates our hearts with melodies of greatness and we praise its magic spell as we have never praised a gift before. Violent at other moments, it switches quickly into threats of frightening disasters and demands from us a price which we pay only to the worst of our enemies. Some see in time a challenge which must be conquered and until this moment of triumph has arrived they are as restless as the pointers of the clock. Others treat the passing hours like a bore, which they would gladly flee if flight were only possible. As a friend time can unfold its wings like a beautiful dream offering to our mind unforgettable memories of the finest hours of our past. As an enemy it is strong enough to hunt us down relentlessly and persecute us until we surrender meekly or collapse in hunger and despair.

Time can afford to move on slowly since it has eternity for its completion. It even possesses a heart and the stroke of its heart is our minutes, days and our years. Noisily, these heartbeats of our clocks step into our life and offer us the precious opportunity to evolve into something better than we were before, or they steal from us, like thieves, the confidence we need to master our fate. Some grasp this offer eagerly and fill it to its very brim whereas others accept it like a rainstorm or greet it like a chilly breeze. Whatever our reception may be, the responsibility is equally grave for all. No one is exempt from giving an accurate account of the use he made of all the hours of his life: "Brief, brief are man's days; thou keepest count of the months left to him, thou dost appoint for him the bound he may not pass. And will thou not leave him undisturbed for a little, till the welcome day comes when drudgery is at an end." [1]

Time is the most neutral power in our orbit. It takes no sides in any battle nor does it bear solutions to a favorite. It never hurried up its path to please the rich and mighty nor has it ever stopped in its advance to hurt the chances of the poor. It is up to us to tame this endless flow of change, as it is up to us to impress on its course the determined message of our mind and will. Our courage, and our courage alone, will shape the face of the tomorrow. To submit to a blind stroke of an uncertain fate is the weakest strategy to gain success and fame.

The clock indicates our worth. Writing down quite accurately our vivid past it assures us that no deeds will be overlooked or perhaps forgotten. Everything we did will be contained in its report, and at the hour of our reckoning, the bills of yesterday are our embarrassing accusers or the best defense we ever had on our side. If we were only prattling idly at the height of the day or staring at nothing at the setting of the sun, then we are guilty of abuse of the greatest natural gift which was entrusted to our concern and disposition. Instead of multiplying precious talents we buried them; instead of gathering rich interests for our Lord, we wasted our substance. The most exuberant source of life turned into the smallest tomb on earth.

Waste of time is however not the only enemy we have to face;

[1] Job 14. 5–6.

delay is equally pernicious. Procrastination is one of the greatest hurdles to success. Many failures and disappointments have their roots in the hours we postponed. By putting off until tomorrow the things we should have done at once, we only placed a heavier burden on new responsibilities. To hope that our duty disappears if we ignore it long enough, this is the hope of fools and cowards. Eventually we have to recognize that the best solution to any given problem is the actual performance. To realize a dream as soon as possible is not only the most efficient way to progress but also the most conducive way to the formation of a sound and balanced character. If we keep abreast of the swing of the pendulum and do what is expected, we will not have to wait too long until success will crown our name and bless our noble efforts.

The language of time is however not always urging to action. Often it extends a gentle invitation to tranquility and peace. Hasty fingers alone will never suffice. Every action must spring forth from contemplation, as every motion must be born of rest. One without the other would only create a stir but never produce an imprint which can endure forever. The monks of old who wrote on their bleak walls — pray and work — knew of the need of inner harmony and silence, whereas we, the offspring of our turbulent century, forget so easily tranquility and peace. Like children we are swiftly fascinated by glaring noise and hasty gestures and we have hardly any use for meditation and for prayers. Absorbed in the excited craving for more activity and movement, we shy away from higher values as they seem futile in the race for bigger profits. Reflection and contemplation are good enough for people in a cloister, but for hardened men in business or politics they only are a subtle hindrance which has to be eliminated before it gets a chance to spoil the earnings of a better day: "And all the while I am the Lord thy God from the land of Egypt; God then shalt own no other, other deliverance is none; out in the desert, out in the parched wastes, owned I thee. Fatal pasturing! With food, came satiety, and with satiety pride, and with pride forgetfulness of me!" [2]

Agitation never has secured salvation. Excitement and commotion alone usually plant no roots in the soil of the eternal city.

[2] Osee 13. 4–6.

The art of waiting, which is so far apart from doing nothing, can lead us to the sources of our real existence. Our modern generation, however, which is perpetually in motion, has neither the desire nor the courage to call its speedy steps to rest. Christ with the greatest mission in history on his mind found always enough intervals to retire into the solitude of the silent night to pray there to his heavenly father, whereas we, busy and perturbed with so many trifles, consider a step into solitude and prayers a regretful waste or a painful luxury. Will we ever grow intelligent enough to judge how immature we are and how conceited?

It is however not only our inner health which profits by the disciplined use of our seasons; there are some other kinds of pains and trials for which time is the best physician. Nothing can heal our wounds so beautifully as the blessed span of a restful year. If the man who suffers grows impatient and alarmed and tries perhaps to push the pointers of the clock to excessive speed, he takes a dangerous risk into his life for which he often has to pay with lifelong misery and desolation. We can accelerate the velocity of cars and make an engine rotate faster; we can propel the wings of our planes to a rapidity far greater than the speed of sound, but we will never be successful if we insist on speeding up the tender healing of a wound. To cure an injury needs time and the most effective medicine we can buy on our markets is the one which many like the least, patience. With patience and with perseverance we will weather many storms and trials, whereas those who only trust their craftiness and deceit will suffer difficulties and defeats: "Patience comes of sovereign prudence, impatience of unchecked folly. Peace of mind is health of body; more than all else, envy wastes the frame." [3]

As soon as we begin to count the blank spaces on the clock of our life we are likely to feel shame and deep embarrassment and a few perhaps even despair. Why did we not use more carefully the gift which was entrusted to our solicitude and care? Why did we have to waste or spoil what is so precious in the sight of God? Have not all of us to admit that we have made mistakes which counted seriously on our total sum of wasted days and years? Who has used every hour to the brim of its capacity? Have we not all

[3] Prov. 14. 29–30.

abused our time and laughed about the impressive number of the days which were our faithful guests, while we did nothing in return? Let us remember, however, to our great consolation perhaps, that not all of those blank spaces could have been avoided. Some of us were unprepared to catch the moment and so the moment did escape. Others again were immature and could not realize the value of the gift they wasted. A few perhaps believed that they were supreme masters of their fate in life, only to find out in the end, that they were hardly anything but slaves.

Time has a different meaning for different people. The selfish ones employ it for the advance and glory of their own productions. Minutes spent for the need of friends are minutes wasted. An hour invested in the care of others is an hour lost. Have we not met the greedy man who never could afford to spare another second? Others however, let us hope many others, are kind enough and willing to share with us their laughter and their cheer and they invite us, again and again, to use their time as if it did belong to us. The worried mother, watching at the bedside of her stricken infant, can she retire at the the stroke of a late hour and call eight hours a full day? Or the doctor, is he allowed to leave the wounded man alone and return to his house because he feels entitled to his rest? Or has the priest the right to say "This time belongs to me alone," as long as others wait for his encouragement and beg for his forgiveness? How different the message is which varied people read from the pointers of the clock! For the one it is a call to sacrifices while for the other it is a golden opportunity to gain more profits at the expense of others. The greedy man will see in time no gift of heaven but plain cold misery in which he has his roots. The humble and the brave however will find in every hour another grace and another blessing: "What you have done to your friends you have done to me."

On few occasions all of us are entitled to turn back the never resting pointers of the clock and relive the history of the years gone by. With nostalgia in our hearts we watch the curtains of old days go up and unfold before our curious eyes the most interesting show on earth, our life! Some watch this spectacle with gloom and sadness in their eyes, and they wish the show had never started; others follow every scene with happiness and joy, and they wish the show would never end. Many fall down on their knees and thank the Almighty for all the innumerable graces which he has strewn so generously on the path of their life, while a few prefer to remain in silence. Yet as different as our reaction may be, no one can justly say, "I have no reason to show gratitude to anyone." "Praise to thee Lord thou has taken me under thy protection, and baulked my enemies of their will; I cried out to the Lord my God, and thou didst grant me recovery. So didst thou bring me back, Lord, from the place of shadows, rescue me from the very edge of the grave. Sing praise to the Lord, then faithful souls, invoke his name with thankfulness. For a moment lasts his anger, for a lifetime his love; sorrow is but the guest of a night and joy comes in the morning." [4]

As much as we like an occasional stroll into the past, it should never become a habitual excursion. To seek solace in the deeds we have accomplished and to forget to seize the challenge of the tomorrow is not conducive to a successful view of our future. To lament the passing of the good, old times is often an admission of our inability to cope with the opportunities of the present situation. A weakling likes to tell us what he has accomplished during years gone by whereas the man of courage will inform us about his activities and plans for the moment which has just arrived. The day on which we begin to dedicate all our efforts to the challenge next on our desk, this very day we have attained maturity. We have grown up, although the number of the years to our credit might still be young and insignificant.

During the time of our pilgrimage on earth we are always strangers, at best exiles from a world which has yet to arrive on our shores of life. We are not allowed to strike roots in a city which is only temporary and which will disappear at the day of the great judgment when Christ himself will finally return to settle his account with all the living and the dead. Until this fearful moment tolls its bells in our harried souls, we have to use the time at our disposal to cultivate and build those values which are exchangeable and profitable in the kingdom which is ruled by God himself. As the monks of old in their beloved deserts used

[4] Ps. 29. 2–6.

their years of preparation to weave some simple baskets only to un-weave them again on the next day, so do we employ our periods of waiting to build some shiny rockets and destroy them again if they fire in the wrong direction. The basket or the rocket does not matter in itself, but the mind and the intention of the performers are the important factors which count so much in the eternal tabulation: "This, too, is the Lord's message: Never boast, if thou art wise, of thy wisdom, if thou art strong, of thy strength, if thou art rich, of thy riches; boast is none worth having, save that insight which gives knowledge of me." [5] The more knowledge and insight we gain into the mysterious world of the divine, the better we have employed our time. The less we learned on this important subject, the less hope is left for us on our day of retribution.

A new year is in the reception room of our life and it waits impatiently for an appropriate welcome. Slowly we approach it, as we approach a stranger whose identity has not yet been fully revealed. A sense of wonder steals into our hearts and stirs up in our curiosity the never silent question "What will this stranger bring to us, what will this stranger offer us?" Many in our midst, as good hosts, usher this unknown guest with joy and celebration into gaily decorated rooms, whereas a few skeptics remain reserved and cool at the presence of this new arrival. No one, however, can completely ignore the year which is so young and yet so mighty. Will it not be the very substance, the raw material of which my life is going to be formed? Will it not be my faithful friend or my severest enemy? Will it not bring to me the answer to all the wishes of my heart?

The rich one naturally expects more money and the poor one naturally expects more too. The healthy one is firmly set to make his body stronger whereas the feeble one hopes for improved vitality. The joyous one is determined to protect the roots of all his happy fortunes, whereas the crying one is eager and alert to still the fountains of his bitter tears. So has everyone his open or his secret wish and the children amongst us write this wish quite carefully on a piece of paper and hide it somewhere in the secret

[5] Jer. 9. 23–24.

153

drawers of the desk, praying that the wish may one day come to life. Everyone wants something,

desires more,
expects more,
craves for more,
requests more,
hopes for more

and few there are who ask "what can I give?"

Have we completely forgotten that it is not the harvest which counts but the heart which throws the bursting seed into the hungry furrow? Was not the farmer whose barns were filled to the brim called by God a fool?

Why was he foolish?

Because he overlooked the fact that he could only keep what he had given away. He amassed so much only to lose much more.

Let us carefully heed the fraternal advice of one of the greatest apostles of all times, St. Paul: "See then, brethren, how carefully you have tread, not as fools, but as wise men do, hoarding the opportunity that is given you in evil times like these. No, you can not afford to be reckless; you must grasp what the Lord's will is for you. Do not besot yourself with wine; that leads to ruin. Let your contentment be in the Holy Spirit." [6]

God himself who is the creator of every new year and the undisputed master of all the hours of our life must come to our help and protect us from our own foolishness and blindness. He has to teach us, with his love and understanding, to seek nothing else in all the seasons of our years but him and him alone. If we seek him now, when we can still find him, we have not to be afraid to lose him when we have no time left anymore to look for him. Only in eternity, when time ceases to be counted, will we be united, at last, with the king of kings who is the beginning of all time and its very end.

[6] Ephes. 5. 15–18.

NINETEEN

The Year Which Never Rests

One of the deepest and most powerful desires in the heart of man is to live a long, long time, yet never to get old. Eternal youth is the alluring wish which swirls through our eager longings, drawing the most captivating pictures to our lively imagination and feeding our subtle dreams with fairy tales and castles. The most fascinating language of the poets heralded and praised this elusive yearning for the fountains of eternal spring while sculptors and painters captivated in stone and colors what man could never fetch with his own bare hands.

Aging is inseparable from the stream of life. As one step follows the other so is one year hastily succeeding the next one. It is not a sudden procedure which strikes us like a flash from heaven but a gradual and continuous one which begins in our body the very day of our birth and ceases only the moment we are laid to rest. We may not even notice it until our hair turns white and our years accumulate; yet long before that moment was age a constant guest in our house. Not that we imply that all of us age in the same intensity or speed — there are variations as different as our seasons — but we assert that in spite of all the differences the last page in the book of life is the same for everyone. When the saddened bells strike their final melody, all our diversities reach the equal level and no one seems to be able to escape this strange equality. It is true that during the race the field widens more and more as some move faster, others more slowly; a few collapse, perhaps, on the wayside and have to be carried while the lucky ones reach the long awaited finishline in a tremendous spurt of speed and vigor. But after the contest is over the winner and the loser receive the same laurels, the jewels of old age.

With pride we are able to assert that so far as we know no other civilization in history has ever reached so high a proportion of people of advanced years as the civilization of our society. Due to our modern hygiene and our potent medicines, thanks to our impressive and growing knowledge we achieved brilliant successes in adding more years to the breath of life and lengthened the race of man for some more miles to go. For this tremendous achievement which benefits us all, we are sincerely thankful and every further announcement about the increased span of life has a personal meaning for us as we should never fail to identify our own future with the present fate of all the aged. Yet as stirring as these joyous tidings sound to our hearts, let us never forget that all our triumphs over time, magnificent as they may be, are of limited character only. The inevitable slowdown can not be avoided and the magic touch which could remodel the weary wrinkles of the face into a stunning beauty has not yet been discovered.

The power of man is destined to decline. It is bound to happen that with the growing number of the years the lustre of life is fading more and more. The force of our decisions commences to weaken and our thoughts, as beautiful as they seem to us, provide less and less originality and persuasion. Even that special talent to make new friends does not seem to burn anymore with the same heat and passion as it did in younger years. With the number of our older friends continuously decreasing, the younger generation seems to be reluctant to take the vacant places nor seem they too interested to share with us the tales of our memories or sing with us the songs of our past. Their time just is not ours and the happenings of days gone by are so different from their newer outlook on life that there seems to be no avenue which links the hearts of these two worlds together. Sooner than we like to realize we find that we are alone.

As in any other machine, the mechanism of our body wears itself out at last and that has its effect on our tired intellect. The memory grows weaker and weaker and our force of concentration which was so keen and vivid is less and less capable of prolonged efforts and of heavy burdens. More than we like we have to confess, with disgust perhaps in our hearts, that we forget so easily what has happened and that we can not remember anymore what everyone else seems to know so clearly. Even our passions, once so fiery and proud, arrive at cooler levels and mellow like a harvest in late autumn. If they were so firmly determined before to rule the waves as a triumphant conqueror, they yearn now more for the gentle gifts of peace and quiet. Slowly but surely the pointers of the clock approach the hours of the evening and all the freshness of the morning remains a cherished memory of many days gone by.

In the same degree however as the outer rind of the tree of life is being worn away, the inner life matures and deepens day by day. The precious seed of grace is far beyond the changes of the law of nature and all the supernatural light in our soul will radiate more brilliantly, the more the cloak of our body wears thin and threadbare. Nothing reminds us more gracefully of our vanishing days of life than the marvelous spectacle of the setting sun. SUNSET . . . there is no beauty more stunning to the eyes of men than this triumphant symphony of colors and of peace. As if the firmaments were caught by flames so are these glowing waves pitching over the red horizon, setting on fire everything which crosses their triumphant course. No wonder that even the heart of the boldest stops for a minute to behold this splendorous outburst of such majesty and beauty. Surely the sun has lost its spark and vigor; yet spending all the stamina of early youth it has acquired such a mellow radiance that nothing is comparable to that late beauty of the evening. Has not the dying sun reserved its most magnificent features for the last? Only now are mountain peaks and meadows covered with the golden glow of glory, and only now assume the rivers and the flowers so delicate a gleam of shadow as we have never noticed on their pretty faces before. Though we are

157

only allowed to contemplate this brilliant display of heavenly smiles, since we are not able to feel anymore the warmth of this celestial message, yet no other meditation kindles in the chambers of our hearts so intense a love as this magnificent exhibit of God's inspired brush. How great must our Master be if his heavenly footsteps radiate such fascinating melodies of peace and grandeur.

Will not the message of our aging years offer us consolations and beauties of the same kind? Will not the calmness and serenity of old age convey to our hearts the same sense of rest and completion which we feel at these late hours of the evening? Have we not met this blessed kind of aged people whose very presence stimulated an atmosphere of joy and quiet? Did we not notice in their sparkling eyes a happiness and smile which were thoroughly cleansed from all the stains of hatred and freed from all the chains of greed? Have we not seen these marvelous aged people whose shell wore thin only to allow the supernatural light to shine more brilliantly than ever before in their long and weary days of life? We met them, yes we met them and we wish to meet them again since we know so well that their meeting was a blessing. Many pages of a book will not reveal to us the precious wisdom which they can teach us in their noble silence and in their measured speech!

But we have met others too. People who advanced in their number of years but declined in the growth of maturity and wisdom. Their shell wore thin, no doubt, but in their aging process they lost the power of the supernatural which alone could keep their precious love aflame until their heart stopped beating. Nothing else seemed to survive in their life but their old age. We expect them to bring peace to us and understanding but we find them restless and exacting. Instead of being eager and desirous to step aside from all the noisy currents of life so that the youngsters have a chance to show their ingenuity and talents, they remain in the midst of all attention and wait for the calls of our rising curtains. Instead of being tolerant and mild, as we would believe them to be after their long and full experience with the temptations of life, we realize that they are very biased in their affections and rather harsh in their critical moods. They guard their petty privileges just at a moment when we would expect them not to be interested any more in our toys and laughters. They start to boast of their rich and glorious past the very moment we trusted that they are ready for the approaching hours of the judgment. It is not rare in such a world of aged people that a whole set of imperfections has survived and that these imperfections and weaknesses begin to command their life the very hour when they should be ready to obey. We have met this kind of old people too and we did not exactly enjoy their company nor did we seek their nearness. If we are sincere, we have to admit that we even tried to avoid their gloomy presence. But if we had to meet them, if no avenue of escape was open, we remember such a meeting as a strain on our minds and our hearts.

Curious perhaps, we like to inquire now about our own future days and the years to come. When will the moment strike on our clock of life when we have to admit that we ourselves begin to age? When will we slow down and look at the speedy youngster without the wish to follow him. It is not only the page of the calendar which provides this inevitable date but also the moment when we begin to watch and scrutinize the customs of our elders and show annoyance about their habits and practices, forgetting so easily that soon we will act in equal manner, if not worse. If we are unduly alarmed by signs and manifestations of old age which are simply inevitable and bound to happen to everyone at that stage of life, we show not only signs of aging ourselves but also portray a certain lack of patience and maturity on our part as well. Is it not one of the easiest things to lose one's patience and to shout if the other party is rather helpless and abandoned? We have to learn now, while we are still sunning ourselves under the wings of spring, to grow and develop inner riches which no thief can steal. Now we have to plant a spirituality which will bloom and flourish in later moments when our hair turns white and our days are definitely numbered. Just as what we learned during the blessed days of our childhood determined the success of our adulthood, so does our growth and development in the middle-life decide the character and stature of our old age. If the seed is not thrown into "the furrow of the propitious time" the harvest will not burst into bread the moment we are hungry and alone. If no attention is paid to the needs of the future now, our aging years may never be a "gold-

159

en age" but turn swiftly into a dark and cursed experience. We fail to gain in splendor what we have lost in intensity: "Do not be afraid, you, my little flock. Your father has determined to give you his kingdom. Sell what you have and give alms, so providing yourselves with a purse that time can not wear holes in, an inexhaustible treasure laid up in heaven, where no thief comes near, no moth consumes. Where your treasure-house is, there your heart is too."[1]

To step away from the contentions of youth and dedicate his experience and knowledge to the task for which he is fitted and adjusted, this is the gracious way to grow in years and wisdom. Every age of life has its own peculiar mental character and strength and the aged man will feel unhappy and discontented if his mind is not in proper accordance with the number of his years. Not many signs are so sad as the sign of a man who does not realize that his behaviour and his actions are those of a child. Surely he is too old to trifle but still young enough to perform. What have left the heart of the aged are only fictions; life however, the real life, becomes more intense than ever before in his existence. Age alone will never exempt or excuse him from finishing the race which has started. Age alone will never absolve him from constantly trying to be the first whenever the winners are counted. History is always on the side of the aged, as it proves without a doubt that more than half of the world's greatest achievements has been accomplished by men who passed their sixtieth year. Not too rarely the triumphal course of a great man begins at an age when the average person retires from the height of his activity into the bore of idleness. Perhaps the first fifty years do provide the text of the book of life while the remaining twenty or thirty years offer the explanations and commentaries without which the book would hardly be understood or treasured. There are still many challenges open where experience counts and where the pressure from younger men, seeking advancement at any price, is not yet felt. These challenges the aged can not disregard or consider lightly as other generations of younger years will swiftly declare him useless or a burden. The society, as it is today, does not award age the credit due to it. The literature, the never-ending

[1] Luke 12. 32–34.

stream of advertising and almost all other sectors of our civilization are of no great help to our aged. They look upon youth as the golden age to which everything else must be subdued and sacrificed. The old are only tolerated but seldom valued or cherished. On the whole the society of our powerful nation is geared and organized to pamper and satisfy the needs of the young, and only slight provisions are made for meeting the needs of the aged. Conscious of this pattern of our society the aged can not expect too much succor and aid from sources outside his world, and he has to rely almost exclusively on the stamina of his own ingenuity and wisdom.

In the centuries past, the aged fitted into the picture almost perfectly. Then they were able to be intensely useful and welcomed, performing necessary services as caring for the flock or herd, fashioning tools and other necessary utensils, spinning on wheels which they themselves had cleverly produced. No wonder that their gentle hands retained their skill and cunning till the moment they could not move any more. Their artful talents helped the family in the unceasing struggle for survival and their counsel and experience aided the tribe in its crucial battle over hostile camps. It would be vain to hope that our surroundings return to the values and customs of the celebrated Middle Ages. With the heightened speed of our modern life, with the burst of our mammoth cities, the radical plunge from an economy based on the skill of hands to the wheels of our humming machines, the aged has been pushed off the bustling main road and advised to find his happiness alone . . . alone in the realm of his friends and in the midst of his blessed family. What was once a cradle has to turn into blessed source of joy and happiness from which the aged can drink until his thirst is quenched. If these sources dry out or if they refuse to spend their "life saving waters," the aged man or woman has no other place to rest. Now many are the tragedies of the old which grow out of the bitter failure to safeguard a response from his family. How terrible the responsibility of a child if he refuses to recognize the desperate needs of his aging parents. It is not the wealth of the child which the aged father or mother desires nor is it influence or any other means of power, but a sincere love inspired by the debt of gratitude; this is all

161

that the helpless heart of aged parents yearn and pray for. If these are not days in which the greater part of humanity indulges liberally in service to others, let us never forget that a divine command was issued by heaven which orders us in strict and simple terms to honor our parents and to obey them. May we never forget that we received from them the greatest treasure we possess ... our life. Rightly we punish the man who betrays the needs and the security of his own nation but we let the man stroll loose who abandons the care of his father and mother.

May we not grow old too early. The heavy easy chair can readily become a source of calamity and idleness for those who close their calendar too hastily. No heroic efforts are required to become a sitter or to kill time while others are anxiously waiting for us to steer their ships through currents and through storms. There are still many fine, strange things to be found and regardless of what we find, the search alone can be a blessing. If youth is a great pile of beginnings, old age might mean a modest number of achievements. The great secret of success is to keep on the alert for our opportunities and never to rest until the rest is forced on us by the inclement elements. Let us never slight the merciful hands of the aged; they have touched so much of life that life itself rests in their hands: "At this time there was a man named Simeon living in Jerusalem, an upright man of careful observance, who waited patiently for comfort to be brought to Israel. The Holy Spirit was upon him; and by the Holy Spirit it had been revealed to him that he was not to meet death, until he had seen that Christ whom the Lord had anointed. He now came, led by the Spirit, into the temple; and when the child Jesus was brought in by his parents, to perform the custom which the law enjoined concerning him, Simeon too was able to take him in his arms. And he said, blessing God: Ruler of all, now dost thou let thy servant go in peace, according to thy word; for my own eyes have seen that saving power of thine which thou hast prepared in the sight of all nations. This is the light which shall give revelation to the Gentiles, this is the glory of thy people Israel." [2]

The dream the aged Simeon cherished all his life came at last into fulfillment. Now he was not only allowed to see the light

[2] Luke 2. 25–32.

which shall give revelation to the Gentiles, but he could also embrace the Ruler of all, the God whom he adored. What else could this world still offer to him? What more could his heart still wish and desire? No wonder that his lips had only one prayer left to say: "Dismiss me now oh my God, for my eyes have seen thy saving power."

The man who ages graciously is deeply aware of the message of eternity. Less agitated or perturbed by the noise of our streets, his soul is more perceptive to the voices from beyond. The approach of infinity lets the reality of time fade away and the path is finally cleared for the triumphal return of Christ, our King and Saviour. With his mind weary perhaps and his lips tired, may he rally once more all the efforts at his disposal and say his last prayer on earth "into thy hands oh Lord I commend my spirit." After this prayer which will sound like his last will and testament, old age which brought us so many sorrows and joys will finally change into never ending youth in heaven.

TWENTY

The Year Which Is The Last

Skulls never do look pretty and they surely look all alike, as if death likes to prove to us that it is thoroughly impartial. Nothing seems to be farther from its mind than preferential treatment of a few. With no exception, we all present an ugly picture in death's unsightly mirror and not even our famous queens of beauty can influence the ruling of this unbiased referee.

The work of death is, without doubt, monotonous, but at the same time it is not unjust. If we have complaints we wish to file against this impartial stranger, it is about its taste and poor imagination. Why do all of us, so varied and so different now, have to appear the same when death engraves its final message into the human countenance? Could there not be some gentle variety and great bargain? As it is now, we just can not get used to looking at faces which death has painted with its bony taste and with its dreadful colors. No wonder that we try so hard to make up for some of the deficiencies by embellishing the appearance of the deceased, so that a person dead looks almost prettier than when this person was alive. One way to answer back to death and make it rather obvious that a better job would not have hurt its reputation. But will death ever change its manners?

164

If we are now convinced that our future picture will not be exactly on the romantic side and if we know so well that all our frantic efforts to beautify our face and body will soon end in a hopeless stalemate, would it not be wiser and more to the point if we were less concerned about the exterior staging of events and shifted our energies and concentration more to man's inner values which, after all, will last a long eternity? Perhaps St. Paul was not so wrong when he reminded us that: "Once this earthly tent-dwelling of ours has come to an end, God, we are sure, has a solid building waiting for us, a dwelling not made with hands, that will last eternally in heaven." [1]

Since hardly anything is less reliable than our momentary looks why spend a fortune, as some do, to improve and adorn their transient appearance? Not that we decry alert solicitude and care, this we recommend and even favor, but excessive attention and extreme concern we intend to criticize since they are purely a waste of our precious time and money. To be content and even happy with features God has given us can bring much greater peace to our hearts than all the fallacies of cheap cosmetics which promise us so much and gain for us so little.

Death has a perfect record; like God it misses no one. No century has hidden yet a refugee from death and we are not at all presumptious if we assert that such a refugee will never come into existence. If there would ever be an island where we could hide from death and flee to safety, this island would be so packed and overcrowded that not an inch would still be free for new arrivals on the scene. What fortunes would the rich ones pay for such high-priced real estate, and how many promises would they not make to be allowed to cleave just to the edge of this fantastic dreamland where tombs would never be of need again. Yet, vain are all these thoughts and foolish because such an alluring island will never find its place on our maps. The rule of death is all-embracing. Its power covers caves as well as all the peaks of mountains; it reaches well beyond the stormy waves of our oceans and even dominates the stars on our firmament. The instant death decides to stop the pointers, no alley of escape is safe and even if we tried to run away behind the wings of utter darkness, we

[1] 2 Cor. 5. 1.

would flee right into its waiting arms: "I know well enough that thou will bring me to the grave at last; it is the home that thou hast appointed for all living men." [2]

If our life is quite an uncertain enterprise and if it is so seriously exposed to the abrupt appearance of its master death, let us be reasonable and calm about the days which are already numbered and use them wisely for those commodities which really count at our end. We can, no doubt, completely waste our time and bore ourselves as much as we bore others, or we can gratefully accept from God the precious gift of our days and invest them well in our eternal bank account. Perhaps the golden road of splendid faith and solid knowledge will curb extremes much better than wishful dreams and ignorance.

Death is not eager to announce its coming in advance. No bell or clock is aware of this important piece of news nor is there any place of information which can predict this great event. Although an undisputed ruler in its kingdom, it frowns on any broadcasted arrival. It likes at best just to drop in and make its presence felt at once. The fewer fanfares and solemnities we arrange for its reception, the more at ease it seems to be.

The kind of welcome WE present to death does not affect its strategy at all. It has its plans and nothing seems to influence its mind or change its judgment. Death keeps its timing to the seconds. Even if we protest most bitterly and beg with our tears for a delay in execution, it carries out its obligation with such perfection that we can only bow our head and weep. The fact that we resent its coming more than we are thrilled by it is no concern to it at all. If we would be prepared, death argues, we would not find its arrival painful. If we are not prepared, however, although we were so clearly warned, we hardly can blame anyone but ourselves alone: "Nor does man see his end coming; hooked fish or snared bird is not overtaken so suddenly as man is, when the day of doom falls on him unawares." [3]

There were however outstanding occasions, in number few perhaps but great in effect, when death had agreed to change its mind and return the booty which was already legally its sure pos-

[2] Job 30. 23.
[3] Eccles. 9. 12.

session. At the command of God, the ruling king of life and death. it willingly released its tightened grip and readily restored to life what was its own for hours only or for days. Even for Christ death had to make this great allowance so that the most important feast on earth "the Resurrection" could take its place in history: "If what we preach about Christ, then, is that he rose from the dead, how is it that some of you say the dead do not rise again? If the dead do not rise, then Christ has not risen either; and if Christ has not risen, then our preaching is groundless, and your faith too, is groundless." [4] Besides these rare exceptions, however, when death acknowledged only its own master, it rules supreme in its domain and shares with no one its decisive powers.

Death honors no insurance policy. Although we are quite solemn in our approach to all kinds of securities, death could not care much less about agreements to which we signed for our death march or the time of our funeral. We pay there and we pay and pay, as if our clinking money could ever buy another hour of this precious life. Some even lay aside a heavy fortune for the very moment when their cold and lifeless fingers can not even hold a penny. How well death knows that poverty makes a departure easy whereas riches stuffed in every pocket make us really slow to look for a decisive change of scenery. While the helpless pauper fears the loss of his immortal soul, the rich is petrified by the idea of losing his accumulated treasures. One hates to be deprived of God while the other is frightened by the thought of failing to win more profits. Both personalities are familiar to death. It has met them through all the centuries and it will meet them again until the end of time. Completely unconcerned about the different amount of gold and silver, it plucks their ready number from the pages of its book and orders both of them to a strict account of their eternal wealth: "Here is one man goes to his death sound and strong, rich and happy, well covered with flesh, his bones full of marrow; another, all misery and poverty, and he no less than the other, has dust for bed and worms for coverlet." [5]

Death has one job to fulfill. It is up to its responsibility to sep-arate the soul from the body and make sure that our strange il-

[4] 1 Cor. 15. 12–14.
[5] Job 21. 23–26.

lusions about the security of this world do not grow deep enough to last. To share with us the formidable knowledge about the pains of hell and all the joys of heaven and make us realize that we are not too sure where we will go, this is the aim of all the lessons it wants to teach us without the help of any book or classroom. What is material in us, death orders back into nature's circulation, while our soul, the melody without its strings, is set free to find its full identity in God. Eternal life does not begin the moment death closes our earthly drama. It commenced the very moment we were baptized to become children of our heavenly father, inhabitants of the city of God. At that great moment of our existence we were reborn for a life which will never end again. Death only changes, but never takes or gives.

Today some stories circulate on our markets, stories which are as strange to our ears as melodies we never heard before. They wish to tell us, in quite serious and learned fashion, that death is not just a beginning but an irrevocable end. To hope that death is only a starting point of our journey to the promised land of everlasting bliss, such hope is vain and useless since behind the darkness of the narrow grave lies no other road to go. Once the lights are extinguished they will never be turned on again. Night is the only thing which surely will be eternal. Beyond the hill of Calvary the sign of resurrection never triumphed. So reads the gospel of agnostics who are so great in their own esteem, yet just a bit too small to fathom the greatness of the thoughts of God. They deny our soul an immortality which God himself has promised us so often, but which they fail to recognize or understand. A life hereafter is only tedious for them. They do not mind to die like beasts, convinced as they must be that such a death is the best their life deserves: "Here is a secret I will make known to you; we shall rise again, but not all of us will undergo the change I speak of. It will happen in a moment, in the twinkling of an eye, when the last trumpet sounds; the trumpet will sound, and the dead will rise again, free from corruption, and we shall find ourselves changed. This corruptible nature of ours must be clothed with incorruptible life, this mortal nature with immortality." [6]

Death is a unique performance. As such it has to be pondered

[6] 1 Cor. 15. 51–53.

168

well and practiced or it will look ugly and distorted. As we can never prepare ourselves for a crucial test just minutes before we take it, so we will never learn how to die in the last second of our life. Such an important event on which depends so much has to be carefully planned in earlier days, in the acceptable time, so that death finds us well adjusted and conditioned when the final hour strikes for the departure.

But how can we prepare ourselves for an event which is so close to our heels and yet so far away from our mind?

The more we become aware of God NOW, the better we are adjusted to welcome death, which unites us only with the object of our intimate longings. If the divine dimensions which are the favorites of heaven are already familiar to us on earth, death will not strike us like a thief, but as a friend who brings to us, at last, what we have long expected and desired: "I have fought the good fight; I have finished the race; I have redeemed my pledge; I look forward to the prize that is waiting for me, the prize I have earned." [7] The only favor we beg of death is time enough to meet a priest. After having met God's representative on earth, we allow death to arrive at any hour of its choice. We are ready and prepared to meet God, face to face, in his own world and under his conditions.

We die alone. Between death and myself no other person is allowed or needed. Interpreters are surely superfluous since death employs a language which everyone can grasp and follow. Others might surround my deathbed and hasten to console me with the best of their emotions, but they are bound to fail in all their noble efforts since I am far ahead of all their thoughts. They can not reach me anymore with all their tales and troubles nor are they able to command my full attention since all my wishes and desires are travelling already on a better road. While they are still quite heavily entangled in their own fears and joys, I am beginning to approach the boundaries of that mysterious land of which I know so much and yet experienced so little. A wise philosopher of the heathens sensed this situation well when he exclaimed: "I go to die and you to live and which of us goes to a better thing, none can tell, save God."

[7] 2 Tim. 4. 7–8.

Frontiers are risky, if not dangerous. At times they even can be fatal to a person who has not studied thoroughly enough the conditions and the climate of their terrain. Reliable information speaks of various territories which are stretched out in front of our eyes and beckon us to settle there and to remain. One is called purgatory, of whose duration we know little but which in many other respects is not too bad a land to dwell. Then we hear about a place called heaven, and how hard it is to find its entrance, in spite of the great crowd of applicants who wish to live and stay there for so long to come. Still another place is mentioned, a place we rather would not speak about if it would not surely exist, hell. This seems to be the hardest territory to get adjusted to, and few there are who really show some interest in its conditions for admittance. Those who are there already would certainly warn us or perhaps even beg us, if they could only speak, not to follow them into this cursed land of the damned, but since we are rarely listening to warnings of this kind it would not help much anyhow.

Which of these different places will be my homeland? Where will I find my eternal place? Will heaven be open for me when I arrive or will God point to the dreadful road of the inferno? Where will I pitch my tent, at last?

These questions are the most realistic ones on the lips of every dying creature. Compared with these burning questions all others disappear from the horizon of our life and dwindles into nothing. If a whole eternity is at stake, the accidental happenings of time lose their importance and sink into oblivion from where they never rise again. God alone, as our judge, becomes the all towering figure who, in his regal majesty, dominates the scene completely. He himself will rule our fate and assign us the place we earned at the propitious time of our preparation: "All of us have a scrutiny to undergo before Christ's judgment-seat, for each to reap what his mortal life has earned, good or ill according to his deeds." [8]

Deeply impressed by the grim reality of this decisive drama in which the whole security of our future life is determined, we find it ever harder to concentrate our thinking or keep our mind in tune with the demands and with the hunger of this world. Al-

[8] 2 Cor. 5. 10.

though still surrounded by the things which were so near and dear to our heart, we feel we lost our share in possession and what remains in our soul are memories of triumphs and of shame. Like strangers, abandoned and alone, we search for the way home and as long as this elusive way is not yet in full sight we are quite restless and perturbed.

Dying people see things as they really are. The mask is off and truth is seen in naked splendor and majestic glory. What we declared as mighty and imposing is prone to shrink in God's evaluation, whereas what God judges holy and impressive was small and poor perhaps in our mind. Real values replace our wishful dreams and what we have so long imagined as the best of our achievements is considered nothing in the mind of God. No wonder that so many people do find God in their great loneliness of death. Disgusted with the flimsy shadows and the mist, they yearn and pray to see the sun, at last. Awakening, more and more, from a world filled with the vanities of creatures, they suddenly witness a scene from which all creatures have disappeared and God has remained the only one to think about. The sharp light of eternity destroys the nightmares of the moments and the hunted soul flees to the safety of the eternal shores where God alone commands the stormy waves and orders us to trust in him, however dark the sky: "It is I, the Lord thy God, that hold thee by thy hand and whisper to thee, Do not be afraid, I am here to help thee." [9]

We can be so frightened by the thought of death that we fail to enjoy the gifts of life. The shadow of the narrow grave can blur the beauty of the setting sun. Some are so terrified by the song of death that no one, in their presence, dares to mention the name of that dreadful skeleton and everyone assumes an air of false security as if our life would last forever. Like children they barricade their trembling souls behind a wall of fictitious safety and hope that death might miss the number of their well-closed gate. "Do not speak of death" is the modern slogan, it will come soon enough without an invitation. Often in the very agony of life, when death moves fast to catch its booty, they continue to play their silly game and gamble on a thing which they can only

[9] Is. 41. 13.

171

lose. Even some of our doctors prefer to speak of life and all its beauties although they know too well that very soon their patient will face death and the approaching judgment. Instead of a clear warning and serious advice, they serve the poison of deceit and claim a deed of kindness where they committed a betrayal. How easily it can happen that such a foolish victim is caught just in the wrong moment, unprepared to answer the questions of the eternal judgment and unqualified to meet God face to face: "You too, then, must stand ready; the Son of Man will come at an hour, when you are not expecting him." [10]

Others laugh about death. They chuckle and they joke as if a hilarious adventure had just come to a stupid end. Dying is a little comedy which they enjoy most heartily as long as others are the lonely victims. To be serious about death and to try to seek the deeper meaning of the message from beyond is far above their understanding and surely against their taste. A shot fired, a knife plunged, poison drunk and a man slumps cold into a dark gutter; that is all. Death is trivial and cheap just like the ugly life which precedes the funeral. Both do not make much sense; both are not worth a second thought. In books and movies, on radio and television murder is the uncrowned hero. Our daily news reports and journals print murder stories as their tragic headlines. Minute descriptions of the savagery of human beings, who seek to camouflage their brutal agony by tearing viciously into the flesh of others, are served our youth as stimulating stories of adventures and as raw material of our modern civilization. As quick and as slick as the whistle of a bullet a precious life is annihilated. Death has to finish the job which was rotten from its very beginning.

Dying has lost its dignity. The immortal soul which makes man so valuable in the sight of God is totally discounted as though it were no more than a helpless leaf caught and destroyed in a never ceasing violence. Some of our frivolous youngsters who see in death nothing but a spreading pool of useless blood are only victims of a cold and brutal atmosphere which some of our entertainers wickedly procure and organize to increase their filthy profits. Added to this "modern entertainment" is the responsibili-

[10] Luke 12. 40.

ty of parents who allow their children to stream to our theaters and movies to see more blood and murders for a reduced rate of admission. If the life of a man is just a little notch on a shiny gun, the life of a nation is not too far away from such a tragic measure. May we reverse this savage trend in our land, before this trend grows strong enough to reverse us and our morals.

Consummatum est . . . it is consummated. On a strange and gruesome afternoon when the pointers of time rested around three, revolting clouds began to dazzle the curiosity of man. The brilliant sun, always punctual for its arrival and departure, gave way to utter darkness. A vague terror took possession not only of the earth and of the rocks which parted far asunder, but also of the baffled mind of men who fled to silence when they began to realize their share of a tremendous guilt.

Such was the dramatic scene which Christ has chosen for the greatest statement of his career and of his holy mission . . . it is consummated, all is now achieved. It was a loud cry, a piercing one which rang through the heavens and earth, a cry which announced victorious triumph over enemies, who just began to think that they had conquered.

The message which Christ brought down from heaven into our midst came at this tragic instant to its magnificent fulfillment. Often our Lord predicted that the heavy price of salvation had to be paid in blood. Now, at this cruel hour, the price was paid in full. An unperturbed Israel was at that very moment engaged in its religious rites not knowing that these same rites had changed in meaning. What they expected for so many centuries had arrived; they knew it now. What had sustained their ancient faith in trials and in persecutions has come into their midst and they received him not. On Calvary, the hill of the cross, one testament turned old whereas the new one, just beginning at that time, became the turning point of history.

If a soldier hears that victory has been won, he forgets all wounds and hardships which he had to endure to achieve this triumph. No one likes to die in vain. Christ looking down from the cross saw Satan's power broken and mankind saved at last. Now he could rejoice because he had accomplished what he came to do. His mission is fulfilled. One thing remained however, one thing still had to be performed before the last page of his book could find its glorious finish: the supreme sacrifice of life itself. Christ lifted his wounded head, raised his eyes and looked through blood and tears towards heaven, saying with perfect confidence and submission: "father into thy hands I commend my spirit." The centurion who represented the disciplined might of the Roman Empire witnessed the scene of Calvary from a nearby point of observation and what he observed was so powerful that he confessed: "No doubt, but this was the Son of God."

Death is a time of harvest. So it was for Christ and so it will be for us. Our achievements will be carefully gathered, checked in real weight and examined by one who makes no mistakes in his appraisal. Our deeds will be searched and scrutinized and not one of our undertakings will be overlooked or forgotten since it made an impression for better or for worse. Our life with its highlights and its disappointments will be exposed to the unbiased glance of death which knows so well what can be brought into eternity and what has to remain in the wastebaskets of our world.

Much of what we have done in life was trash. Although we advertised so many deeds as "done for God alone," we realize in these precarious moments that we only used the name of God as a pious label attached at random to our dealings in this world. Now, under the impending pressure of the imminent departure, all our labels melt and crumble. Only deeds of love and self-effacement remain after the scrutiny of death has passed.

Consummatum est . . . it is achieved. I, too, have to make this statement. May the supreme surrender of the greatest gift I possess, my life, be an acceptable holocaust to you, O Lord. Please, O God, accept the offering of my life now and do not hesitate to receive it. You were always the desire of my heart, believe me, even when this, my heart, was too feeble to bear the greatness of your love. You guided me so gently and so firmly and yet I went so far away from you, only to be found again by you, who never lost a sinner. You know the roads I went and all the clefts into which I stumbled and yet you always followed me to bring me back again to the tabernacle of your Love. You never abandoned me; you never let me go. Why?

Now, hunted by death, I fall down on my sinful face at the

174

feet of your holy grace. I, the unprofitable servant, whom you endured so long, I bow deeply into dust from which I am made and beg with my tears for your mercy. With all my sinful speech I approach your eternal stillness, hoping against all hope, that I have achieved in my life what you expected me to do.

It is consummated. The song of my life has reached its final melody. What I wanted to say to you, I have said. You have to speak to me now; it is your turn. Please, tell me, at this greatest moment of my life, what I yearn to hear from your holy lips; tell me now that I am saved, saved by your inexhaustible mercy, saved by your infinite love. Tell me now, O Lord, that death is for me a sign of resurrection into a life of everlasting glory.

So be it, O Lord,

so be it,

Amen.